THE Upside OF Downsizing

KAREN O'CONNOR

HARVEST HOUSE PUBLISHERS

EUGENE, OREGON

Cover design by Dugan Design Group, Bloomington, Minnesota

Cover illustration © Dugan Design Group, Bloomington, Minnesota

Published in association with the Books & Such Literary Agency, 52 Mission Circle, Suite 122, PMB 170, Santa Rosa, CA 95409-5370, www.booksandsuch.biz

THE UPSIDE OF DOWNSIZING
Copyright © 2011 by Karen O'Connor
Published by Harvest House Publishers
Eugene, Oregon 97402
www.harvesthousepublishers.com

ISBN 978-0-7369-2861-8

Printed in the United States of America

11 12 13 14 15 16 17 18 19 / BP-SK / 10 9 8 7 6 5 4 3 2 1

To my parents, Phil and Eva O'Connor,
masters of the cozy lifestyle,
which they shared generously throughout
their 60-plus years of marriage.

Acknowledgments

Thank you to the many friends who
participated in this conversation
about downsizing.

Contents

PART 5: Trying Things That Don't Come Naturally

PART 6: Simplifying with Shortcuts

PART 7: Building an Inner Life

PART 8: Living Fully

Embracing a New Life Season

Reduce the complexity of life by
eliminating the needless wants of life, and
the labors of life reduce themselves.

EDWIN WAY TEALE

Some people dread downsizing, viewing it as a step back from life, the beginning of the end. They worry that younger people will overlook or neglect them. They wonder if they will matter as much as they once did. And they're concerned that now that the active parenting days are over they no longer have purpose. "How will we fill our days?" they ask. Others embrace this new season with joy and expectation, eager to chuck their stuff, simplify their lives, relax, and focus on the important—their relationships with God and people. They're eager to continue to make contributions to the world in new and creative ways.

This time of transition can be the perfect opportunity to toss the junk we no longer need or want (and sometimes wonder why we bought in the first place). We can move into smaller, more intimate spaces, where we'll have more hours to read and rest and travel and garden and whatever else we discover we enjoy. Why not kick back or kick up a storm of new activities—the kind we never had the time or resources for before? We have less to handle, less to think about, less to clean. We have more time to explore, help others, and build stronger relationships.

> "Shut the door. Not that it lets in the
> cold, but that it lets out the coziness."
>
> **MARK TWAIN**
> *NOTEBOOK, 1898*

Downsizing can spell r-e-l-i-e-f instead of fear or sadness or regret. This can be a time with space to relax, to tuck in, to look out for ourselves, and to set positive examples for others on what it means to live fully. My husband, Charles, and I are in such a space now, and we love it. Our kids are grown and making lives of their own. They're now the ones with the packed basements and garages, big backyards, attics, and storage bins. More power to 'em! We had all that—but no more. We're now all about living in the moment, no longer hemmed in by possessions we have to clean, fix, and maintain.

There *is* an *upside* to this season of life! A side that is all about peace and joy, rest and simplicity, order and comfort, warmth, and relaxation. A side that calls out for cozy, easy living free of clutter and chaos. Let's explore some downsizing options and discover the many upsides to entering this wonderful time of life. We can enjoy what we've already accomplished and look forward to many great experiences as we embrace life on the other side of 55.

Karen O'Connor

Part I

TAKING THE PLUNGE

What Does Downsizing Mean?

I have enjoyed greatly the second
blooming...suddenly you find at
the age of 50, say, that a whole new
life has opened before you.

AGATHA CHRISTIE

Three years ago my husband, Charles, and I moved to a small community along the Central Coast of California. The homes in this neighborhood were built for people 55 and older. As Charles said, "We're more than qualified." As we became acquainted with our neighbors we noticed that, like us, they had downsized—not only from larger homes but also from hectic lives. We all agree that it feels good to be close to beautiful farmland bordered by foothills alive with birds and giant redwood trees. It's so quiet at night I can hear the crickets even with the doors and windows closed. And the moon and stars decorate the sky in a way I didn't often see in the well-lit city we moved from.

Downsizing for me has more to do with *atmo-sphere* than square footage. I relish the peace and silence my new life offers. We also have a guest room for the first time. Now my adult children and grand-children can visit for extended periods or come and go as their lives permit. Our home is a haven of love and hospitality for us and them now that they have moved on and created lives of their own. Charles and I are creating a cozy lifestyle that suits us per-fectly at this stage of life.

A friend and I were recently discussing buy-ing things for our homes. She said, "I don't need another item. In fact, I'm trying to get rid of the clutter, not add to it." For her that's the essence of downsizing—living a simple, spare life that opens up time and space for *doing* and *being* rather than accumulating and storing. I'm with her!

Another upside to downsizing is discovering it's okay to say yes to only those activities you really want to participate in and say no to those you don't. This is a learning process, and I'm having some suc-cess already. I searched out a knitting class near my home and joined. I've wanted to knit for more than 40 years! I also found a suitable hiking group through the Sierra Club that I thoroughly enjoy.

Why not...
> hunker down for one hour today and
> simply be?

Downsizing means different things to different people. What does it mean to you? What do you imagine a cozy life would look like? You now have more freedom to create the schedule and live in a location where you can flourish during these happy golden years. Why not jot down a list of the kinds of people, places, and things you'd like to have in your life now that your kids have moved on?

The glory of young men is their strength,
gray hair the splendor of the old.

PROVERBS 20:29

Making and Keeping Friends

If you make it plain you like people, it's
hard for them to resist liking you back.

LOIS McMASTER BUJOLD

Downsizing often means letting go of the old
and taking on something new, including new
friends, especially if you move to a different neighborhood or city. I remember being worried that I
wouldn't be able to find *my* people when we moved
north. I was leaving behind 40 years of life in Southern California. I couldn't imagine being able to
duplicate or replace the solid friendships that had
taken so long to build. But then I realized there
are hundreds of good people wherever I go. I meet
them all the time. They will find me, and I will find
them. I became excited about the possibilities.

And sure enough, I wasn't disappointed. I met
my first new neighbor and friend the day my husband and I walked through the model homes in

the community we chose. Ruth and her husband, Mike, had selected the same floor plan we had, and our houses were across the street from each other on the only cul-de-sac in the neighborhood. Ruth was my kind of gal. And so were Shirley and Carol and Bev and Rose. Within weeks we were chatting in the street and over fences, walking on the levee together, enjoying potlucks and games through the homeowners' association gatherings. At our ages we didn't have decades to build our friendships, so we started from where we met and moved forward.

Today I am so grateful for these dear women— sisters in every sense of the word. I can call on them; they can call on me. We're in this new cozy life together. I've also stayed in touch with my friends from my "old" life in San Diego. I telephone, e-mail semiannual newsletters, and mail brief updates at Christmastime. We get together a couple of times a year so we can enjoy each other's company in person. Those friends will always be in my heart even though they're not in my everyday life.

Why not...

connect with one new person today through a smile or handshake?

Making new friends and keeping the old is part of a happy and healthy life, so pay attention to both. One of the upsides of downsizing is the blessing of people—good, caring people wherever you land. They'll find you, and you'll find them.

Do not forget to entertain strangers,
for by so doing some people have
entertained angels without knowing it.

HEBREWS 13:2

Downsizing with Purpose

A goal without a plan is just a wish.

ANTOINE DE SAINT-EXUPERY

I received a phone call from a woman I'd met at our new church. She welcomed me to the congregation and asked a few questions that helped us get acquainted. Then she asked, "Would you be willing to..." and shared a list of opportunities for volunteering that was long, intriguing, and tempting. However, I had made a deal with myself: *No commitments* unless they were in line with my *purpose*. I declined all the woman's opportunities. My husband and I had moved to be closer to our youngest daughter. She and I hadn't always lived together during her young adult years, so I was grateful for the opportunity to be near her now, especially while her children were young. And I was still youthful and healthy enough to be useful.

My mission field was my family. With fewer

things to distract me now, I could focus on what I felt was God's purpose for bringing us to the Central California Coast. And the changes were easy to accept once I was clear with my goals.

Charles and I have created a life for ourselves, as well. We aren't dependent on our daughter and her family, and they're not dependent on us, even though we've made each other a priority. As I drive the kids to school or to the park or dance class or play rehearsal or soccer, I feel connected to them in a special way. We have time to chat, tell jokes, sing songs, and pray together. I feel warm and cozy inside. I'm not simply doing an errand. I'm building a lifestyle and relationship with these young people that I hope will influence them positively all the days of their lives. They have already done the same for me.

Why not...

> focus today on *one* thing that really matters to you?

So when anticipating downsizing, or if you have already taken the plunge, consider discovering your primary *purpose*. This will be personal to you. Then stick to it and notice how sparkle and warmth fill your life. Cutting back, slowing down, paying attention, focusing on what really matters will bring you a richer, deeper, more satisfying life than you ever imagined.

> *Do what is right in the Lord's sight,*
> *so that it may go well with you.*
>
> Deuteronomy 6:18

Getting Finances in Order

Never spend your money before you have it.

THOMAS JEFFERSON

How can putting your financial house in order lead to a cozy life? By taking the burden of *thinking about it* off your mind. Plus you'll be reminded of what papers you have, you'll know where everything is, and you'll be able to cull out the outdated and nonessential items in your files.

Another great benefit is that we can give our children a file folder or binder with copies of all of our important papers, from a Trust or Last Will and Testament to medical records, bank accounts, and contact information. They'll also get the names of key professionals we've worked with: physicians, attorney, accountant, pastor, funeral director, business partners or representatives, and close neighbors and friends who can provide current information to our families and help them if we become disabled or our health fails.

In 1991 my husband and I put together a three-ring binder with copies of everything we had at the time, from birth certificates to our wedding license, from our prepaid plan for cremation to our plan for the disbursement of our assets. We also included a contents page listing the items in the book so our kids could put their hands on specific documents easily and quickly. We were proud of ourselves for taking this important step.

At the time we planned to update it every year. But we didn't follow through until January of 2004, when we sat down and organized our affairs once again. First, we created a Family Trust with the help of an attorney who specializes in such matters. Then we looked at every paper and document we had filed away, updating where appropriate and tossing out when possible. After that we created a comprehensive list of what was left.

Next we wrote a letter to our grown children expressing our wishes and intentions, attached the list of documents and where to locate them, and then made a copy for each one and sent them off via Priority Mail. What a relief to know they will be able to take charge when the time comes.

There is another upside to this type of downsizing. As you let go of things, you can also let go of worry and fear and resistance. Do what's necessary to give yourself and your children peace of mind. Then focus on what you love—family, travel, sports, reading, music, and gardening.

Why not...

treat yourself to one small luxury today that doesn't cost a penny?

If you're ready to do something to get your finances in order, consider how you wish to disburse your estate, who will be in charge, and which professionals will be helpful to your family and friends. Allow enough time to think through all aspects of these issues. It won't happen overnight or even in a few hours. It's worth setting aside a weekend, for example, or a couple of evenings when you and your partner can get together to discuss the issues. You might even want to meet with your children with the exclusive goal of discussing and organizing the information. Personal history, medical conditions and preferences, and financial facts are among the most important details to be considered. You may want to compile a notebook like we did or create a computer disk with the information.

I remember reading about a woman in her sixties, widowed at the time, who put all of her documents and wishes in order, passed out copies to her three children, and then told them she was off to see the world in the time she had left.

Later her daughter reported that her mother enjoyed a wonderful decade of travel before she died. "I miss my mother," she said, "but I'm so happy she used her retirement years in a way that was pleasing to her. She left a legacy of wonderful memories, as well as a notebook of well-organized documents that made it easy for my siblings and me to put her affairs to rest without going crazy. I want to do the same for my children when the time comes."

Whatever you have learned or
received or heard from me, or seen
in me—put it into practice.

PHILIPPIANS 4:9

Living with Courage and Enthusiasm

No matter how old you are, there's always
something good to look forward to.

LYNN JOHNSTON

It all went by so fast," Maureen said. "Now the boys are grown and out on their own. Our house is so quiet. Not that I'm complaining, mind you." She chuckled. "In fact, Jack and I are rather enjoying it. But still I miss our kids being around. All three are in different cities doing their own thing. I feel like shouting, 'Hey, we're here! Don't forget us. We're your support team, remember?'"

I could relate. I felt that way after our children established their own lives and married. We so enjoyed their visits, but I was sad when they left. It might be weeks or months until we got together again. I longed for the daily comings and goings and all the little details that I was in on when they were still living at home.

It takes courage to face this new chapter in our lives. Downsizing isn't always voluntary or easy. Kids leave home and it's just us now—the two of us—the same two who were eager at times for this period of life to arrive. But now that it has, we miss the good old days. Or maybe you were a single parent so now it's just you at home. That can be an even bigger adjustment.

It also takes courage to make the most of the days that lie ahead. One great fuel for moving forward is enthusiasm. Without it, we can become complacent, accept the status quo, and let our memories swamp us. Every season of life is special in its way and holds its own gifts, but sometimes we need to discover the new form in which they come.

Why not...

greet the day with expectancy—rain or shine?

Perhaps the most important thing we can do as we downsize is to be generous with ourselves, meaning be patient, loving, appreciative, and supportive. God is with us, and he will never leave or forsake us. Resting in that truth will provide the comfort and strength we need to carry on when life changes.

I find that doing something each day for someone else, as well as for myself, puts me in a happy and contented frame of mind. I'm giving and receiving, serving and being served, loving and being loved in return. With such blessings all around me, how can I not survive *and* thrive. And the same can be true for you.

> *Wait for the LORD; be strong and*
> *take heart and wait for the LORD.*
>
> PSALM 27:14

Part 2

GETTING FREE!

31 Simple Ways to Joy

Real joy comes not from ease or
riches or from the praise of men, but
from doing something worthwhile.

SIR WILFRED GRENFELL

One of the ways we free ourselves from nagging thoughts, worries, regrets, and annoyances is to focus on joy. This may take practice, especially if this virtue doesn't come naturally to you. To help leave the negatives and focus on the positives, here are 31 simple suggestions. Why not do one or more a day? And, of course, feel free to substitute something better if it occurs to you. You can also repeat the actions you enjoy. Perhaps these will also spark ideas suited specifically to your interests.

- Invite a new neighbor in for tea and conversation. Get acquainted!

- Meet a friend or colleague for a lunchtime walk. Exercise and conversation are a great combination.

- Give your spouse a foot rub or a back massage before bed to help him or her unwind (the next night could be your turn).

- Walk barefoot on the grass in early morning— an invigorating wake-up call to your body.

- Take a break and have a cup of your favorite brew and a big, fat muffin. Sit a while and reflect as you sip and chew.

- Visit a bookstore and browse the shelves. Pick a book that's just right for this moment in your life. Buy it, take it home, and read it!

- Call someone you haven't seen in several weeks or months. Reconnect.

- Send a note, a greeting card, or an e-mail to six people in your address book just to say hello and let them know you're thinking of them.

- Take a leisurely salt bath and then a nap.

- Buy a bouquet of flowers or even a single rose. Place it on your desk or dresser where it will provide color throughout your day.

◆ Jot down all the blessings you received today. Revisit the list a week from now and remember how rich you are.

◆ Purchase a medley of fresh fruits and make a big fruit salad. Feast on this healthy food and notice how good you feel.

◆ Call your parents (or someone who has mentored you) and tell them you love them, even if the relationship has been rocky at times. You're alive because of them, and that's something to be joyful about.

◆ Stand in front of the mirror and declare out loud two positive things you notice about yourself.

◆ Take a positive risk. For example, tell someone a constructive truth you've been withholding or compliment someone you admire.

◆ Volunteer at a local hospital or clinic, get active with Girl or Boy Scouts, interact with a church youth group, or take part in local government.

◆ Be creative. You can bake a fancy cake, arrange dried flowers in a pretty basket, sew, knit, make jewelry, draw, or build something.

◆ Start a "joy journal." Every day write down one thing you have to be joyful about.

Why not...
   pick one of the simple ways to joy and do it
   with gusto?

◆ Plan your summer vacation, and then take one step toward making it happen.

◆ Buy a new set of bed linens in a bold pattern or color that makes you smile.

◆ Toss or give away the clothing you haven't worn in the past two years.

◆ Enroll in a class for fun, such as cooking, needlepoint, ice-skating, or cake decorating.

◆ Veg out! Take time to sit and stare into space. Enjoy the moment.

◆ Drink eight glasses of water today, and notice how great it feels to be fully hydrated.

◆ Smile at everyone you meet. Pay special attention to the ones who smile back.

◆ Allow someone else to have the last word, even when you deserve it.

- Listen to classical music while driving.

- Ask for help when you need it. It's a joy to be able to share a burden.

- Reconcile your bank account. Oh the relief you'll feel!

- Comfort someone in need.

- Say or write an original prayer of thanks for a month of joyful new discoveries and reflections.

Rejoice in the LORD, you who are righteous, and praise his holy name.

PSALM 97:12

Make Peace

First keep the peace within yourself, then
you can also bring peace to others.

THOMAS À KEMPIS

"I am so frustrated with Dave," Greta confided recently after a challenging weekend with her husband. And I have to admit that I understood. From my perspective Dave was a handful. He liked to do things *his* way or no way. And now that he and Greta were retired and had moved to smaller quarters, the friction had escalated.

Everyone comes up against difficult people and circumstances in every area of life—marriage, families, friendships, and work. We can't avoid them completely, but we can do something about them. And no, I'm not advocating divorce or moving out of the neighborhood to get relief. Relationships don't break down overnight, and they don't become restored in a matter of hours either.

First, start with prayer. I'm convinced God wants us to find common ground with even the testiest people in our lives and then reach out to them with love and understanding. Here are some other steps that will help you in this difficult area.

Take Advantage of Your Differences

The strong personality wants things done now and can't understand why he (or she) can't have his way immediately. The reflective person wants to think things through and look at all the options before making a decision.

If we view these differences as assets instead of difficulties, they can work *for* us. Look for the talents and gifts in the other person and work with them instead of resisting and judging them. For example, suppose your neighbor is a controller and can't seem to stay out of your business. You wonder, *Can't she see how annoying she is when she tells me how to make my plants healthier?* Apparently not. Therefore, take the lead by thanking her for her ideas and then giving her a role in that area of her strength. Ask for her help in planting your roses. If she struggles with her family, invite her to join you in reading one of your favorite books on parenting or grandparenting. Chances are she needs positive attention and opportunities to be useful.

Communicate Without Being Confrontational

Recently, someone I respect very much taught me a couple of important phrases that I've incorporated into all of my intense conversations: "I'm sorry that what I've done hurt you" and "I could be wrong." Neither one diminishes me. Both give me the opportunity to dialogue so the two of us can share our hearts and come to agreement about what to do next.

Face Your Flaws with Humility and Humor

My mother-in-law enjoyed telling our family about an incident early in her marriage. Her young husband made life difficult for her—especially in the kitchen. "No one can cook like my mother," he'd say often.

"I decided to fix him," Ada said with a glint in her soft-blue eyes. "Instead of arguing and defending myself, I enrolled in a cooking class. I became a good cook and he never complained again. I gave in and he gave up." A touch of humor helped them over this rough spot.

Create New Ways to Relate

Most of us get stuck protecting, promoting, or defending our behavior instead of looking at what doesn't work, why it doesn't work, and what we can do to get the situation working better. People who want to heal difficulties are willing to toss out the old plans and draw up new ones. Go to the person you perceive to be difficult. With sincerity and honesty introduce a new element into your relationship that will show your willingness to do whatever it takes (within reason) to live in harmony with him or her.

Why not...
> whisper a prayer of peace for one difficult person in your life?

Look to God As Your Source of Healing

To live on the *up*side and to experience a close and cozy life with those we love, we have to be willing to do our part in bringing about the harmony we seek. With God on our side, we can't go wrong. He is in the relationship business. He wants peace and understanding among us even more than we do. And he'll direct our feet if we will listen and then follow him.

If Nothing Works…Let It Go for a Season

And if you try as many alternative ways to approach or deal with the difficult person as you can think of and there's still a problem, let the relationship rest a while. Quietly pray about it and let God handle the situation.

> *What I have said, that will I bring about;*
> *what I have planned, that will I do.*
>
> ISAIAH 46:11

Hang On to Your Moola

If you would be wealthy, think
of saving as well as getting.

BENJAMIN FRANKLIN

Some people love to save and others love to spend, whether it's a couple of dollars for a coffee and croissant or a slice of pizza and a bottle of pop. Each of us can do a few small things to hang on to more of our hard-earned money. The secret is to give in *once in a while* to our small passions, such as going to a movie, purchasing a new CD, buying a pair of earrings, getting the latest handyman tool, or indulging in a new book. These little pluses are part of creating a cozy life and are definitely one of the *ups* in downsizing.

A few days before Valentine's Day, Charles and I shopped for food. We'd agreed not to purchase gifts for the occasion since we had a weekend trip coming up the end of the month and wanted to save our cash for that. As I perused the bread aisle, Charles meandered over to the fresh flowers. He came back and pulled me gently toward the display.

"See this bouquet of beautiful yellow roses?"

"Yes, I agree, it's lovely."

"This is what I *would* have bought you," he said with a wry smile, "but I didn't because of our agreement."

"I receive them for the moment," I said, and I gave him a hug.

Why not...
> linger over something beautiful in a store, but leave without buying it?

We both laughed and finished our shopping. We drove home and settled in to watch the Olympics and enjoy the snacks we'd purchased. Ah, the benefits of growing older and not having to answer to the cultural commands and demands. I loved it! And we saved 20 bucks by admiring the flowers in the store—and leaving them there.

Here's another idea. How about eating at home more often? Many retired folks dine out several times a month, but even when you catch the early-bird special or take advantage of a senior discount at your favorite restaurant, you'll still spend at least $20 to $50 for two meals. The dinner may be a modest charge but add an appetizer, beverage, coffee, and dessert, and you've racked up a bill. You might decide, instead, to eat out one night a month or save such an expenditure for special occasions only, such as a birthday, your wedding anniversary, or Valentine's Day.

When you do go out, think about sharing a meal (if you can agree on what to order). When two share there is no waste and the price is right. Less food and fewer calories are better for your waistline and your wallet.

Also consider why you want to go out to dinner. Is it because at home one of you does all the cooking and cleaning and wants a break? Or does one of you do the cooking and the other person does the cleaning? Why not do both jobs together for a change? You can visit and laugh as you work side by side. And maybe you'll discover, as I have, that eating at home can be more relaxing than eating out. Charles and I watch a movie or catch up on conversation while we dine. And we don't have to get dressed up or fill the gas tank.

What other ways can you think of to have fun while hanging on to more of your moola?

> *Do not wear yourself out to get rich;*
> *have the wisdom to show restraint.*
>
> PROVERBS 23:4

Guarding Against Isolation

To resist the frigidity of old age one must
combine the body, the mind and the
heart—and to keep them in parallel
vigor one must exercise, study and love.

KARL VON BONSTETTEN

I've been alone too much," my friend Reenie
said one day as we visited over coffee. "I know I
should get out of the house more, but sometimes it
takes too much effort even to get dressed."

Reenie and her husband, Ed, had recently sold
their family home of 35 years and moved to a retirement community in another state. They had
grand expectations of what was ahead of them—
new friends, interesting opportunities, entertaining
events for seniors, being within walking distance
of a golf course and shopping center. What more
could they want?

After settling in, however, Reenie's mood plummeted. She'd left good neighbors, a caring church family, and familiar surroundings. She missed them all. Her solution? Stay home and "veg," hoping the negative feelings would pass. But they didn't. Instead they deepened.

Why not...
 invite a neighbor on a walk?

It takes courage to step away from the people and situations we've known for decades and to give ourselves to something new. Even giving up some of the clutter that has held us captive can be scary. But the upside is that we'll eventually have renewed energy as we take on the risks of *elimination* (ridding ourselves of junk we no longer need or want) and *participation* (stepping out and encountering new people and situations).

My husband and I recently joined the University of California at Santa Cruz's Lifelong Learners program (LLL). Their website states Lifelong Learners is "a community of men and women from diverse educational, occupational, and geographic backgrounds who are devoted to the pursuit of learning. The members enjoy spirited discussion, reading, and exploring new interests." It's been great for us.

I encourage you to look into educational programs in your community that give you opportunities to acquire new friends and experiences. When we downsize the amount of stuff we have and instead accumulate knowledge and solutions, we'll be uplifted in body, mind, and spirit. Think about what you can do to avoid isolation—and then step out and do it!

Trust in the LORD with all your heart and
lean not on your own understanding;
in all your ways acknowledge him, and
he will make your paths straight.

PROVERBS 3:5-6

Choosing Experience over Possessions

By far the best proof is experience.

SIR FRANCIS BACON

I'll take an experience over an item every time," my friend Peg said one day as we were shopping in the mall. "I know we have to buy food and clothes and household items, but when I have a choice, I'll opt for a concert or a play."

I agreed with her then, and I feel even more strongly about choosing experiences over possessions now that I'm older. Charles and I have everything we need in most categories. And our wants are few at this stage of life.

We've shared this with our adult children too. A good telephone conversation or a walk along the ocean together means more to me than a new thingamajig for the garden or kitchen. A new pair of earrings or a soft scarf is lovely, but given my druthers I'll pick doing something that inspires my spirit and brings joy to my soul.

Why not...
> sit in the sun for five minutes with your eyes closed? Savor the warmth!

I know Charles shares this sentiment, so for his birthday this year our family went to a state park on Monarch Butterfly Day and enjoyed looking at these lovely creatures that return to Santa Cruz every October. Then we went to a quilt and photography exhibit to see the works of some of our artistic friends, followed by homemade chili and a delicious cake at our daughter's house. The grandkids created cards for the occasion, which meant more to Charles than a gift in a box with a bow on top. It was a lovely and memorable day, and it was all about experiencing time together in nature.

This is a delightful aspect of the *up*side of downsizing. We now have the time and the willingness to *be,* instead of distracting ourselves with projects and new possessions. And we hope we're setting a

good example for our children and grandchildren
to follow as well.

> *In [the LORD] our hearts rejoice,*
> *for we trust in his holy name.*
>
> PSALM 33:21

Part 3

CHANGING PATTERNS

Pitch the Clutter

Organizing is what you do before
you do something, so that when
you do it, it is not all mixed up.

A.A. MILNE

I have suits and skirts and blouses and more shoes than I'll ever wear." My retired neighbor Norma smiled in embarrassment as she told me about finally purging her closet of clothing, footwear, and jewelry she no longer needed or wanted. In fact, she wondered aloud why she had moved them to her new, smaller house when she could have pitched them before the moving van arrived. "This is just one more symptom of my unwillingness to face my stuff and then organize what's left," she admitted.

That seems to be the case with many people, especially as we get older. It's a lot of work to sort through boxes and closets and shelves and then make decisions about what to do with the inventory.

We develop a pattern of saving for a rainy day or holding on to certain fashions hoping they'll come back into style or we lose ten pounds. Meanwhile our closets bulge, our garages get overcrowded, and our minds are overwhelmed with what to do and not do with our stuff.

Why not...
toss or give way one item you no longer need, want, or use?

I remember my mother begging my dad to unload his collection of old magazines before they moved from the family home to an apartment after he retired. He resisted. "I might want to look through them again one day." That day never came. Ultimately Mom removed them all before their final move to a retirement center.

My friend Kate's mother met an attractive widower in her later years. They fell in love and the man proposed. Kate's mom said yes under one condition: He had to get rid of all the cancelled checks, bank statements, and other documents he'd been holding on to since 1960. He did—reluctantly.

Don't allow clutter and chaos to rob you of joy and peace. Finish what you've set out to do, and then treat yourself to a special experience. Get organized, and the rest will fall into place.

> *[The LORD] will teach us his ways, so*
> *that we may walk in his paths.*
>
> ISAIAH 2:3

Divvy Up Treasures

As we bless others, we bless
ourselves as well.

KAREN O'CONNOR

I remember one night having dinner in my parents' apartment. My chair faced Mother's china cabinet. As I sipped my tea, my eyes lingered on the lovely hand-painted dessert plates my grandmother (who had died before I was born) had given to Mom. I remarked how beautiful they were. "I hope some day you'll pass one on to me," I said.

"You can have them right now," Mother responded. With that she popped out of her chair, opened the cabinet, and pulled out all six. "Take the one you like," she said, obviously thrilled that I liked and wanted them. "And then pass out the others to your sisters and daughters." Before I left town that week, I'd packed the plates carefully in my suitcase. Now *my* plate is on a display shelf in our "family museum," a glass-front cabinet in our living room.

Mom had entered the downsizing time of her life and was more than happy to divvy up some of her treasures so the next generation could start enjoying them. I want to do the same. I've already begun thinking about what to give each of our children. In fact, I spoke with an attorney about this, and she suggested we find out what our sons and daughters specifically want and then make a list of the items with their names by them. A friend of my mother's did something a little different. She decided to whom she wanted to give the family heirlooms and then put stickers on the bottom or back of each item with the child or grandchild's name.

Why not...
give away one small treasure today?

Of course we don't want to strip our homes too soon. We want to enjoy what we have and hopefully we'll be around for another decade or two. But if you're ready to downsize, now might be an ideal time to pass on some of those treasures. Be aware that perhaps some of your treasures won't be considered wonderful by some of your family members. My husband's aunt saved every piece of furniture, trinket, and doodad. By the end of her life, her rooms rivaled an antique shop. She'd hoped her grandchildren would want to take things off her hands when they married, but they didn't. They had their own tastes and ideas of how to decorate their homes. So be judicious in what you save and what you deem treasures. And if you have a treasure your family doesn't appreciate, don't be offended. Instead, find someone who will like it.

The secret is to find a happy midway point—holding on to a few treasures that add to enjoyment but also freely giving to our loved ones as they express interest.

> *Your plenty will supply what they*
> *need, so that in turn their plenty*
> *will supply what you need.*
> 2 CORINTHIANS 8:14

Surround Yourself with Beauty

Order is the shape upon
which beauty depends.

PEARL BUCK

My husband and I love paintings, especially watercolors. When we travel, we visit museums, cathedrals, and galleries. I remember a time we walked the streets of Carmel, California, going into one gallery after another. It was such fun—and it didn't cost a thing. As we paused for a coffee break I remember telling Charles that I had just saved us $20,000.

"You what?" he asked.

"I tallied up the costs of all the paintings I saw that I'd love to have in our home," I explained, "and it came to $20,000. Of course I didn't buy even one!"

We laughed and went on our way, having enjoyed several hours of beauty that added something special to our day.

The artwork on our walls at home is primarily copies and prints, though we do have a few originals by a friend. Nonetheless, all are beautiful and were within our budget.

Charles and I also enjoy flowers. Every spring as new blooms poke out of the soil I feel a ripple of excitement. I know that soon our garden will be filled with vibrant colors in various shapes and sizes.

I appreciate another kind of beauty: order. When things are in place I'm peaceful and happy. For instance, it's important to me to make our bed each morning. As I pull up the quilt and bedspread and prop the pillows against the headboard I'm reminded of the day we bought the bedding and how excited we were to decorate our bedroom with such lovely textures and colors.

Beauty shows up in myriad ways. Paintings and flowers and a made bed are just three. I also love to take walks in the park, in the mountains, and along the seashore. God's creation trumps all the rest.

Why not...
freshen your home with a scented candle?

What experiences and objects are beautiful to you? Why not make a list? Then think about other beautiful things you don't usually consider or haven't thought of before now. Take steps to include them in your life, whether they be concerts, movies, strolls in meadows, a new set of dishes, a lovely vase, a pretty item for your home, or a new tool for the shop.

As we take our eyes off the mundane and rid ourselves of clutter and confusion, there is room and time and space for the experiences and things that warm our hearts, lift our spirits, and expand our appreciation of the beauty that is life itself. Isn't that a cozy thought?

*The house of the righteous
contains great treasure.*

Proverbs 15:6

Give Them Away!

If we have the opportunity to be generous
with our hearts, ourselves, we have no idea
of the depth and breadth of love's reach.

MARGARET CHO

Yard Sale!"

"Garage Sale!"

"Moving Sale!"

None of these signs motivate me to hold one. I don't like the work involved: setting things out, arranging them in related groups, deciding on prices, tagging each item, collecting money, making change, and sitting outside all day while people come and go and pick through my belongings.

I prefer what I consider the easy way: *Giving my stuff away!* To the Salvation Army, Goodwill, Purple Hearts, or other charitable organizations. Twice a year Charles and I gather the books, clothes, shoes, and household items we're finished with and drop them off at a nearby charity.

Why not...
give away one item you love but don't
need today?

This pattern has also helped us pay more attention to what we purchase. The things we think we
need or want today usually become tomorrow's dis-
cards. So now we are more conscientious about our
shopping sprees. We enjoy walking through a store
and then giving each other high-fives as we leave,
recounting how much money we "saved" by not
purchasing any of the things we admired.

We've given away luggage, camping gear, sweat-
ers, shirts, shoes, and a used car. We've gifted a desk
to a young colleague at work, furniture to a con-
struction worker in need, and gardening tools and
miscellaneous kitchenware to a refugee family we
befriended. We can't take our things with us when
God calls us to heaven so we might as well lighten
our load and live a simpler, cozier, clutter-free life
now while we have time to enjoy it.

What do you say? Want to join us?

Give, and it will be given to you.
LUKE 6:38

Keep It Simple

As you simplify your life, the laws
of the universe will be simpler.

HENRY DAVID THOREAU

I recall a transforming moment in my life about 15 years ago. I read in Elaine St. James' bestselling book *Living the Simple Life* this timely advice: "In order to simplify, we have to start making choices, sometimes difficult choices." As I continued reading, I realized that like Elaine and her husband, Gibbs, Charles and I needed to make some new choices about the people we socialized with, the groups we attended, the activities we participated in.

We needed to determine what really mattered and what didn't. If we wanted to simplify our lives, it was time to let go of a whole bunch of stuff, from worn-out relationships to worn-out clothing. We needed to learn to say no (politely, of course) to invitations for events that didn't interest us.

These things took some doing, but we did it. And we're much more peaceful and happy for having done so. I stopped going to Mexico to help in an orphanage. We declined learning how to ski even though our skiing friends thought it a great way to spend weekends. And we gave up eating at fancy restaurants. It was costing too much, the portions were too large, and more times than not we liked our own cooking better than the chefs' preparations.

For so long I did many of the "right" things for all the wrong reasons, including trying to please God without talking to him about it, looking good to others, and trying to feel better about myself. What I now know is that when I respond with honesty and integrity, I'm being true to myself *and* to God. I hope my life is an example to others of the peace and joy that can occur when we realize our limitations and expectations of ourselves and others and live accordingly.

Why not...

let go of one social commitment you've outgrown?

Do I still do good in the world? I hope so. I write and speak and teach—all of which are true to my

God-given core values and talents. I'm involved in the lives of my children and grandchildren. I knit and hike and cook and garden and share the fruit of my endeavors with others.

The blessings of the simple life, at least for me, can't be overestimated. Now when I am asked to join this group or that, to attend this event or that one, or to get involved in a cause or benefit, I stop, check my spirit, whisper a prayer for guidance, listen for the reply, and then make a decision.

I'm keeping it simple, and I'm inviting you to do the same.

> *I know what it is to be in need,*
> *and I know what it is to have plenty.*
> *I have learned the secret of being*
> *content in any and every situation,*
> *whether well fed or hungry, whether*
> *living in plenty or in want.*
>
> Philippians 4:12

PART 4

HAVING FUN

Dance!

Dance is the hidden language of the soul.

MARTHA GRAHAM

Just as there's a time to weep and a time to laugh, a time to mourn and a time for most everything under the sun, according to the Bible there's also a time to dance (Ecclesiastes 3:4). The trick is knowing which time it is and realizing it can be different for different people.

On one New Year's Eve there was a musical tribute to the great Ella Fitzgerald presented live at Lincoln Center in New York City. I was watching it on TV and Charles was watching and listening from the kitchen, which is only partially separated from the living room. I remember Ella from the 1950s when I was in high school and college and a devoted fan of jazz. When I heard some of her familiar tunes again, such as "How High the Moon," "Dream a Little Dream of Me," "The Man I Love," sung by such notables as Nancy Wilson and Natalie Cole, I suddenly felt young again.

I wanted to hold the man I love, dream a little dream with him, and gaze out the window at the moon high above. But it didn't seem to be the right time for romantic activities. There we were—me without makeup and in my old sweats and Ugg boots, hair askew, eyes squinting through glasses that needed a good cleaning. I'd restored my house that day after the holiday guests had gone but hadn't yet pulled myself together.

Meanwhile Charles was putting away food and dishes from dinner, scrubbing pots and pans, and commenting here and there on the music and the memories it evoked. "That was a great era. They don't write love songs like those anymore."

Suddenly I knew what time it was—a time to dance!

I looked at Charles and smiled. "Dance with me?"

"Now?"

"Um hmmm." I stood and held out my arms as I swayed to the music.

"But I'm in the middle of—"

"I'm in the middle of something too—of a longing to dance with you."

"Okay." He walked out from behind the half-wall that divided the kitchen from the living room and took me in his arms, a sopping dishtowel over one shoulder, an apron around his waist.

I put my left arm on his shoulder—the one without the wet towel—and fit my right hand into his left one. He pulled me close, sweatshirt to sweatshirt, and danced me all over our new hardwood floor that seemed made for dancing. The faux flames in the faux fireplace licked the faux logs as we whirled and twirled, I in my Ugg boots and Charles in his.

Why not...
grab your partner and dance right now?

In my mind I was wearing silver strap stilettos and a close-fitting black dress with pearls around my neck. Charles was clad in a navy-blue suit with a white shirt and cuff links, black Ferragamo loafers, and a smashing red-and-blue-striped Robert Talbot silk tie.

"We won't forget this night," I teased. "When one of us is gone the other will remember the New Year's Eve when we danced the night away in our Uggs and didn't care a hoot about it—as long as we were holding each other close."

He nodded in agreement and smiled behind eyes wet with tears. I realized that for Charles it too was a time for dancing. He just hadn't realized it until I held out my arms.

And so we danced and danced and danced.

[There is a time…] to dance.

ECCLESIASTES 3:4

Vacation at Home

The alternative to a vacation is to stay
home and tip every third person you see.

AUTHOR UNKNOWN

You've heard the expression "There is no place like home." Dorothy said it after returning from Oz, and many seniors are saying it after coming home from trips abroad that left them weary and cashed out.

Airfare is up and the cost of fuel is off the charts. The price of a restaurant meal has increased. So what is today's senior traveler to do? Put the expenses on a credit card and deal with it later? Or give up vacation plans and settle for TV?

I suggest a third option: a "staycation." I first saw this word in an article by Melanie Wells in *The Wall Street Journal*. She was referring to a stay-at-home vacation she and her family enjoyed one summer when they were in the midst of moving from one residence to another. They had fun together without packing a suitcase, standing in line at airports, and changing time zones.

I've experienced this type of vacation as well. When my children were young and we were strapped for cash, my husband and I decided one summer to be creative. We looked at what it would cost to house, feed, and entertain our family of five for a week away from home. It was a bundle! And that didn't include boarding the dog and paying someone to water our plants. We realized that if we slept in our own beds, ate breakfast at home, and brought a picnic lunch to eat on the road, we could still have a great time on a slim budget.

As I look back now it was one of the most enjoyable vacations we had. We lived in Southern California at the time, so we focused our attention on the attractions that were within a two-hour round trip from our home. One day we toured the historic Queen Mary ocean liner. The next day we visited the LaBrea Tar Pits. We spent time swimming at a local club and playing tennis. Another day we went to a park, took a long walk, fed the ducks in the pond, and enjoyed a picnic of all our favorite foods. The last day we went to Disneyland. By the end of the week everyone was onboard to do something similar the following year.

Now that I'm a senior and a grandmother, I'm inclined to do the same thing with my husband, daughter and son-in-law, and their family. They live close by, and there's so much to do right here on the Central Coast of California. The Monterey Aquarium is less than 30 minutes away by car. San Francisco is about 90 minutes north of us. We could spend an entire day or two there visiting Ghirardelli Square, the zoo, Muir Woods, and Golden Gate Park.

Why not...
do something today that shouts "Vacation!"?

On staycations, part of the fun is the planning. Consider things you wouldn't generally take the time to do when you're involved in your routine. Douglas Trattner, in an article on home-based vacations for *Fine Living*, suggests buying a guidebook for your city and then following a one- or two-day itinerary. You will likely find places and activities you didn't know existed. Your local convention and visitor's bureau or an automobile association can also be of help. Need some more suggestions?

◆ Take a bus tour of your city. Maybe you live in New York City and have never seen the Statue of Liberty. One of our senior friends lived in New York his entire life but he never saw Lady Liberty up close until he was an adult and took time to visit the sights in his own city. Is there a museum, historic house, English garden, or performing arts center in your community that you've never explored? On a staycation you can visit one or all of them.

◆ Choose a restaurant that offers a bit of entertainment as well as good food. Some of the Japanese eating places seat patrons around the grill so they can watch the chef chop, cut, cook, and perform tricks with cooking tools that dazzle the eye. Though the meal can be a bit pricey, you probably won't mind if it's the main event for that particular vacation day. We found that two people can share one order and still have plenty of food. Children enjoy restaurants with themes, such as Corvette Diner, Hard Rock Cafe, Farrell's Ice Cream Parlour & Restaurant, Bar-B-Q Bill's, and Rock & Roll Diner.

◆ Take a shuttle, commuter train, or bus to a sporting event. Make the transportation part of the fun. While riding you can rest, read, play a magnetic board game, work a puzzle, enjoy music on your iPods, or just talk with your family. You'll arrive at the game feeling refreshed. And you don't have to worry about parking!

* Create a serendipity day. You may find, as I have, that it's nice to reserve one day for whatever— for whatever comes up. A simple breakfast, a stroll in your neighborhood, a leisurely drive through the country, or simply hanging out at home. My husband turned to me on such a day and said with a smile on his sleepy face, "It's so nice to wake up knowing we can do whatever we want today—maybe even nothing."

If you're looking for a way to have fun at home, consider the benefits of a staycation. Lisa Oppenheimer, a Boston-based travel writer, sums it up this way: "With a little creativity and planning we can duplicate that feeling of relaxation without ever leaving our hometown."

I agree. Why not give it a try?

You will go out in joy and
be led forth in peace.

Isaiah 55:12

Take a Hike

I dream of hiking into my old age.

MARLYN DOAN

One summer my husband and I joined a group of hikers for a trip to the Eastern High Sierra. Such an adventure was new for us, and we were excited about what lay ahead. We packed our gear according to the leader's specifications, prepared our bodies with daily walks and pumping iron at the gym, and gathered our dried food, bottled water, and hiking poles. Off we went to meet the team at Red's Meadow in Mammoth, California. We loaded our duffel bags on the mules that were waiting to take us to our destination.

The first day we met an older man who appeared to be a veteran hiker, an expert compared to us since this was our first trip of this kind. I was eager to talk with him about his experiences. I wanted to learn as much as I could about the wilderness, what to enjoy, what to avoid, what to expect.

He sat down on a chair in front of our tent one morning to chat over a cup of coffee. The sun had just pierced through the tall pines and splashed across the green canvas, warming our faces and hands and casting a lovely glow on the meadow beside our campsite.

"So what prompted you to start hiking?" I asked. "I'll bet you've been at this for years. We're a bit late in taking on this hobby—I'm 55 and my husband is 65, but we hope to carry on for years to come, just like you." I babbled on, hardly breaking for a breath.

Stan looked at me and chuckled. "Don't give me more applause than I deserve," he said. "I'm not that far ahead of you on the trail. I turned 70 this year, and I didn't start until I retired from IBM five years ago."

Why not...

take one morning or afternoon to hike a local park, shore, or foothill?

I looked at my husband and winked. He was starting at the same age as Stan had. I leaned in closer and asked a few more questions. Stan seemed to enjoy the attention. Finally he answered my initial query about his motive for starting in the first place. A smile curled his lips and a twinkle lit up his blue eyes. "My wife gets the credit," he said. "When it came time for me to pick up the gold watch and the last paycheck at the firm, she panicked. What would she do with me around the house all the time? She didn't realize it then, but one command from her lips was all it took to set me on the trail. 'Go take a hike!' she said one day. And I did!"

The moral of the story? If you want to do something, do it. If you don't know how to get started, ask someone who's gone before you. Join a group or club, meet like-minded people, and then go for it. You never know what wonderful new adventures you might encounter. See you at the top!

The mountains and hills will burst
into song before you, and all the trees
of the field will clap their hands.

ISAIAH 55:12

Schedule a Play Day

Live and work but do not forget to play,
to have fun in life and really enjoy it.

EILEEN CADDY

Several years ago I read *The Artist's Way* by Julia Cameron. One of the suggestions she made was to treat yourself each week to a day alone doing something you love. "Can I invite my spouse or best friend to join me?" someone asked. "No! That's not part of the deal," Cameron said. The point is to spend time with yourself. I liked the idea, but I wasn't sure I could go through with it. At first it seemed a bit self-indulgent, maybe even a waste of precious time. Why do something by myself when I could do it with another? Wouldn't that make it more fun? Maybe...but then maybe not.

I decided to play by Julia's rules. The first week I signed up to attend an open rehearsal of the San Diego Symphony. It was pure delight. I listened and pondered and enjoyed the music instead of whispering my emotional responses and observations to a companion.

The following week I drove to the Carlsbad Flower Fields and walked several miles up and down and through the paths between each planted area. The fragrance, the colors, the warm sun on my face, the breeze in my hair blessed my soul. I couldn't wait to go back.

Why not...
> pick an activity you love, put it on the calendar, and then do it?

In the weeks that followed I found something special to do without even trying. In fact, I had so many ideas I wondered if I could fit them all into a 52-week year. Sometimes my choice was as simple as parking along the ocean and sipping hot tea from a thermos while I prayed and listened to the waves crashing on the shore. Other times I visited art museums and stayed in the rooms with my favorite exhibits as long as I wanted to. The more dates I had with myself, the more I enjoyed my own company. I returned home feeling peaceful, satisfied, and filled with joy.

After nearly a decade I've mastered the habit. As you eliminate the activities in your life that no longer matter, you'll be free to add those that do. A play date with yourself is a delightful way to enjoy the *up*side of this time of life. I encourage you to give it a try!

> *Now may the Lord of peace himself give*
> *you peace at all times and in every way.*
>
> 2 Thessalonians 3:16

Surprise Your Mate

The moments of happiness we
enjoy take us by surprise.

ASHLEY MONTAGU

My husband is fascinated with the story of newspaper magnate William Randolph Hearst. He's talked about the man and his life many times over the years and has visited Hearst Castle on the Central Coast of California more than a dozen times. Charles is also more than a little interested in railroads since he comes from a railroad family. His father was an electrician for the Illinois Central Railroad Company. I'm sure if I bought a toy train to encircle our Christmas tree my husband would be as thrilled as any six-year-old.

With these cues in mind, I decided to surprise him with two special dates. For his birthday one year, I arranged for us to ride the Roaring Camp Railroad through the Redwood forest in Felton,

California. As the literature boasts, it is "a journey back in time to Redwood forests echoing with train whistles." Charles even met the engineer. What a thrill for this 80-year-old boy.

This year for Christmas I set up another surprise date. I booked tickets for the Christmas Evening Tour of Hearst Castle. This too was a step back in time. The castle docents dressed in period clothing, resembling the fashions Hearst and his guests wore during their heyday in the 1930s. The rooms were beautifully decorated for Christmas, and the various costumed "guests" played their parts well in the billiard room, the parlor, the dining room, and so on.

Charles' eyes sparkled and misted as we strolled through the castle following our guide, who shared fascinating facts and trivia about Hearst and his era. We came down from the hillside satisfied and happy. I'm so glad I took action when the thought occurred to me.

Why not...
surprise your mate with a date that matches his or her interests?

These kinds of surprise dates were simply not

possible years ago when we were raising a family and so focused on the kids' activities and needs. But now that we're in the latter half of our lives, we have more time for one another and a few extra dollars here and there so we can indulge ourselves.

Life passes so quickly. I'm realizing more and more how important it is to make the most of the time we have and to add a bit of zest to it by surprising my mate with special dates that will mean so much to him.

Light is shed upon the righteous
and joy on the upright in heart.

PSALM 97:11

Part 5

TRYING THINGS THAT DON'T COME NATURALLY

Go Back to School

Education is the movement
from darkness to light.

ALLAN BLOOM

My friend Marilyn decided to go to law school after her last child left home. She was 50 at the time. Two people commented that she'd be 55 or older by the time she graduated, got a job, and started to build her practice. "Why bother?" seemed to be the prevailing attitude.

I admired her response to the naysayers. "In five years I'll be 55 no matter what I do, so I might as well be 55 *and* be an attorney at the same time." And so she enrolled in law school. Today, nearly 20 years later she's a partner in a law firm.

Wes and Donna had time and money on their hands after their children moved out and met and married their spouses. "I've always wanted to own a piece of land where I could see something grow,"

Wes said. He and his wife drove to Northern California, purchased a vineyard, attended classes on the art and science of growing grapes, and now sell their harvest to local wineries. They found the *up*side of downsizing by realizing a lifelong dream that required both education and application.

Wendy barely made it through high school, married young, raised a bunch of kids, some her own, others through foster care, and when her youngest left home she was worn out and bereft. What was next? She had no direction, yet she was only 53 years old. She decided to enroll in a memoir writing class at a nearby junior college in order to explore her life and feelings. Within a few months she produced a 125-page rough draft of her personal story. "Maybe no one except my teacher and I will read it, but that's okay," said Wendy. "I put my life on the page, and I'm excited to see where I'll go from here."

Why not...
> enroll in a class—whether carpentry or cooking, fashion or flower arranging?

These are just a few of the folks I've spoken with about the *up*side of downsizing. Instead of settling in for the last few decades of life, they decided to further their education by going back to school or taking classes.

You don't have to head for a BA, MA, or PhD. You may wish to take classes in topics that interest you: art appreciation, novel writing, painting, film, music, or woodcarving. It doesn't much matter as long as you're using your time in a way that satisfies you and carries you forward. It's never too late to begin something new, and there's no time like the present to give it a try.

He gives strength to the weary and
increases the power of the weak.

Isaiah 40:29

Get a Prayer Partner

One single grateful thought raised to
heaven is the most perfect prayer.

G.E. LESSING

Years ago I invited a woman I met at church to be
my partner in prayer. I was new to the faith at
the time and newly divorced. She agreed. Her marriage was over as well, and she was as devastated as
I was. We've been praying together now for nearly
30 years!

I also have a prayer partnership with one of my
writing colleagues. We've been giving and receiving prayer for one another for at least a decade. Our
books and articles have been the main focus, but we
also pray for personal and family needs.

And finally, I have a "heartner" (our code word
for "partners of the heart"). Lynni and I support
each other wherever needed with lots of love, special prayer, listening ears, advice when solicited, and
empathetic silence when it's not.

Sometimes being a prayer partner can take you to the brink. One more step and the relationship goes over the cliff. But still, you *have* to take the step of honesty and forthrightness. You have to be willing to risk or you're not a true partner—you're an accomplice! I remember a time when I spoke my heart (and mind) to a friend about her decision to marry a man I didn't trust. My friend defended her choice. She married him and stopped speaking to me—for a time. Today she's divorced…and we're friends again.

I also recall a time when a woman spoke truth in my ear. She showed me how complaining was pulling me down in every area of my life. "You have a lot to be grateful for," she reminded me. "Start noticing the gifts—and give thanks in prayer." I listened, reluctantly at first, and then willingly. And my life changed from one of "If only…" to "Thank you, Lord, for this new day and all it holds for me."

Why not...
find a prayer partner today and start praying together?

We all need individuals in our lives who *care* enough to *be there* in the trivial, in the trials, *and* in the triumphs. J.I. Packer, in a chapter on prayer in his book *Knowing Christianity,* reminds us that we should not forget "the special benefit of praying with a like-minded Christian who is committed both to God and to you...happy then is the one who finds such a partner, and stupid is the person who never seeks one...It is good when we can travel two by two."

And there is no time like right now, in our later years, to move *up* in life with a partner in prayer.

> *Before they call I will answer; while*
> *they are still speaking I will hear.*
> ISAIAH 65:24

Opening Your Home and Heart

The most important work you
and I will ever do will be within
the walls of our own homes.

HAROLD B. LEE

My husband and I plopped down on our new outdoor furniture, iced teas in hand, and admired our handiwork. Our condominium was freshly painted inside and out. The flowerpots were brimming with pink, white, and purple blooms.

"We can't keep this to ourselves," Charles said. "How about inviting some friends over while the weather is still warm and the days are long?"

"I'm willing if we can keep it simple so we can enjoy it too."

"Agreed," he said.

We made a list of friends and neighbors, jotted down some tentative dates on our calendar, and then planned ways to make the get-togethers festive and fun. Here are a few ideas we came up with. Perhaps they will work for you too.

Soup 'n' Salad Party

This is a nice way to break up the week without requiring too much time and energy. July and August are ideal months to serve this light fare. A soup with summer vegetables, a make-your-own-salad bar, and no-bake cookies add up to a complete meal. Your dieting friends will also appreciate this menu.

Pancake Brunch

This is one of my favorite ways to entertain. Chef Charles flips pancakes from griddle to warming pan. I top each stack with homemade applesauce, a sprinkle of freshly ground walnuts or pecans, and whipped cream. Serve with coffee, tea, or juice. This is an easy and inexpensive meal that appeals to everyone. After breakfast we walk to a nearby park where we sit around and talk.

Dessert Buffet

Homemade cheesecake, hot apple slices, crunchy macadamia nut cookies, lemon tarts. A feast for everyone with a sweet tooth. Invite as few as four or as many as twenty neighbors, friends, family, and coworkers to join you for a buffet of sweets and coffee, tea, and lemonade. Ask each couple or individual to bring a favorite dessert and the recipe printed on three-by-five cards to share with other guests.

Why not...
invite another couple or a single friend to join you for a shared meal or activity?

Movie and Popcorn Night

Pick a favorite flick from your neighborhood rental store or choose one from your own collection that would appeal to a certain couple or group of friends. Set up the living room or family room with comfy chairs and small tables for holding snacks and drinks. When your guests arrive, spend some time chatting and then announce the name of the film and usher them into the viewing room. Bring in the hot popcorn, bowls of nuts, and plates of small crackers with squares of cheese. Set up a tub of ice-cold soda, water, and juice and encourage your guests to help themselves. Settle down for the show.

For a festive and fun summer, open your home

and heart to the people you love. As you share yourself, you'll be sharing God's love as well. Now that's definitely an *up*side to any phase of life.

> *Each one should use whatever gift*
> *he has received to serve others.*
>
> 1 PETER 4:10

Try Something New

*You have to recognize when the right
place and the right time fuse and take
advantage of that opportunity.*

ELLEN METCALF

I can't wait to retire!" Alice's husband, Ed, proclaimed. "I'm going to plop in front of the TV and that's it. Chips and Coke and the remote," he joked, "are all the companions I need."

I wondered how Alice felt about such a declaration. I imagine she had some ideas of her own. And from the sound of it, whatever she might have wanted to do she'd be doing on her own. How sad. Lots of people fall into the same trap. They figure they've worked all these years, and they deserve to sit out the rest of their lives. But does such resignation produce happy results? I doubt it.

If you've always wanted to hike a mountain, quilt a comforter, try out for community theater, learn to ski, join a bowling league, or go bird-watching, you can do it *now*. And if the activity you want to try is new to you, so much the better. There's nothing like an untried adventure to invigorate mind and body.

After my kids left home, I took up hiking—as I've mentioned earlier—something I'd wanted to do since I was a girl of six. I'm proud to share that I've made it to the top of Mount Whitney!

I turned around my failed first attempt at knitting by starting again—almost 50 years later. This year I finished knitting six scarves to give to the women in my family for Christmas. I may even try a sweater next.

Why not...
push your fear aside and do one small thing today that takes courage?

Charles wanted to test his mettle at public speaking—something he never had enough time for during his early working years. For the last decade or so he's had a more flexible working schedule so he joined Toastmasters International. Now in his retirement he is having the time of his life refining his speaking skills. He's also been a guest judge for regional and state speech competitions for school-aged children.

Trying something new can have its downside, but only if you're afraid to fail. As long as you're willing to step out in faith along with hope and a sense of adventure, you can have the time of your life and inspire others to do the same.

Trust in the LORD and do good.
PSALM 37:3

Mend Fences

The creative adult is the child
who has survived.

URSULA K. LEGUIN

Downsizing can present plenty of challenges. Moving to smaller quarters is one of them. There's so much to face, to discard, to save, to give away. But you can solve such problems once you put your mind to it.

Some of the really big problems aren't in the practical realm. They're subtle, emotional, and relational. They have to do with our *children*—our adult children. One of the *up*sides of downsizing life in terms of housing, career, and lifestyle, is the opportunity you have to resolve any residue of conflict you may have carried regarding your children and the way you parented them.

"Mom!" my daughter exclaimed over the phone. "I can't believe it. I shamed Brandon. I said I never would—but I did. I was so irritated with him I lost control. What should I do now?"

"Oh honey," I responded, "I know the feeling. I never wanted to make that mistake with you either. I loved you so much I couldn't imagine lashing out— yet I did. Go to him right away and apologize. It's never too late to start over. Remember when I…"

As I shared a similar experience from her childhood, we both laughed. It wasn't funny at the time, but we could smile about it now.

Why not...
call or write one of your adult children and express your love?

After speaking with my daughter that morning, I was aware again of the wonderful grace God gives parents—a second chance, a fresh start no matter how many mistakes we made or make. Like the apostle Paul said, sometimes we do what we don't want to do, and we don't do what we say we want to do. We can't wipe out our wrongs, but we can acknowledge them to God, to ourselves, and to our children. We can apologize, ask for forgiveness, and then roll up our sleeves and start again with a clean slate.

I was also filled with the reality of God's love

for each of us. He gave us a second chance through Jesus Christ. *Surely, such a loving Father wants to redeem our parenting too,* I decided.

Turning to God

Talking about a second chance, however, can be quite different from living it. I can think of numerous ways I've failed: being impatient with a child who needs a little extra time to tie his shoes, getting angry over spilled juice cups, being irritated with little girls who fuss about clothing and little boys who don't care enough about what they wear. None of us has been the perfect parent. But God is with us, guiding us to make things right. Here are some things I've learned by the grace of God. Perhaps they will encourage and help you.

Admit Your Wrongs

Repent, then, and turn to God, so that your sins may be wiped out, that times of refreshing may come from the LORD (Acts 3:19).

Trust That Honesty Will Build Healthy Intimacy

I know, my God, that you test the heart and are pleased with integrity (1 Chronicles 29:17).

Face Your Flaws and Failures with Humility and Humor

Who is wise and understanding among you? Let him show it by his good life, by deeds done in the humility that comes from wisdom (James 3:13).

Release Your Mistakes to the Lord

Those who know your name will trust in you, for you, LORD, have never forsaken those who seek you (Psalm 9:10).

Restoration is not for the arrogant or the prideful. It is for people who are willing to admit their faults and to bring them to the Lord for healing. It is for parents who want all that God has for them and for their children.

As far as the east is from the west, so far has he removed our transgressions from us.

PSALM 103:12

Lead Your Grandchildren by the Spirit

A grandchild fills a space in your
heart you never knew was empty.
AUTHOR UNKNOWN

I remember as a child standing outside my grandfather's bedroom door watching him seated at his desk and reading from an old black book—the Bible. I realize, now that I'm a grandparent myself, how the Word of God filled him up, guided him through the trials he endured, and refined the rough places within him. The result was a gentle man who had a bright smile, a kind word, and a loving hug for everyone who knew him—right up to the day he died. That was my first introduction to Scripture—and it led the way to a close and personal relationship with my grandfather that lasted until his death at age 90. As I reflect on those special times, I see what a tradition he laid down for my life simply by being a good example.

I want to make that same investment in the lives of my grandchildren. And now is the time to do it, when they still like to hang out at my house, spend time with my husband and me, and *listen* to us. You might be having similar experiences with your grandchildren.

Kids of any age are quick to notice a sermon in disguise, so it's important to guard against spiritual manipulation. We don't need to tack on a Bible lesson to every conversation we have with them. There are dozens of opportunities available for spiritual interaction—if we keep our hearts open to the Holy Spirit. We might share a simple Bible lesson one day and go on a walk the next, play a game of tag one moment; comfort a crying child with the Lord's Word the next. When our lives are in tune with the Spirit, our responses will be appropriate.

Maybe your grandchildren aren't being raised in Christian homes. Or their parents express disinterest or disapproval when you talk to their children about the Lord because they feel it's the parents' responsibility. Sometimes just living a faith-filled life in front of our families is witness enough. Other times the Spirit may lead us to speak openly about our faith when the right opportunity comes along.

Why not...

    invite one grandchild on a just-the-two-of-us outing?

I had such a time this week while driving my teenage granddaughter to school. She was weepy and sad over an incident in her life, and she'd had a bad night with an injury to her neck. As we drove, a verse came to mind. Isaiah 54:17 says, "No weapon forged against you will prevail." I laid a hand on her arm and shared with her the power of these words and then suggested she repeat them throughout the day when she felt overwhelmed. She thanked me, and I left it at that. Small gestures such as this can make a difference even if we don't see it right away.

Regardless of our circumstance, I believe the Lord calls grandparents to be involved with their grandchildren's spiritual development and to share their faith without fear. Now that we have the time and the opportunity, let's take advantage of it. A cozy, peace-filled life is one that points to God as the author and finisher of all things.

Children's children are a crown to the aged.

PROVERBS 17:6

PART 6

SIMPLIFYING
WITH SHORTCUTS

Think Small

We improve ourselves by victory over our self.
EDWARD GIBBON

Bigger is better." "Don't belittle yourself—'be big' yourself." "Think big." With all the press about thinking big and being big and doing big things, it might be hard to imagine there is value in thinking small and doing small things. But there is. And when you're finally retired, there couldn't be a better time to practice it.

Consider the wisdom of the following actions and how they might lead you toward a simpler, cozier, less stressful life.

Take Small Steps

When you're sorting through your possessions and wondering what to keep, toss, or give away, think small. Go through one closet, one drawer, or one cabinet at a time. When you're comfortable with that increment, proceed to the next small goal.

You'll be more relaxed and less apt to make decisions you might regret later.

Allow Small Mistakes

It's easier to clean up a cup of spilled water than a bucketful. Small steps cut down on the effects of mistakes. And if you make one, it's not a big deal—it's just a small one. You can make necessary corrections simply and easily. A miscommunication, a misstep, a misunderstanding is more likely to be noticed when you're not overwhelmed. You'll have time to correct it. Think small and take small steps with people, as well as things.

Take Small Time-outs

When you feel fatigue setting in or anxiety gripping you, don't pile into bed and pull the quilt over your head. Stop what you're doing immediately. Cut off the stress and fatigue *before* they get the best of you. Think small: stretch, smile, sip water or tea, nibble on some fruit or nuts. Take a small walk or a short nap. You'll return to your routine refreshed and ready to continue.

Notice Small Increases

As you learn to think small, you'll also notice

small changes. Your confidence will heighten. You can learn a new computer program after all. You'll meet new people more easily. You'll surrender old obligations so you can investigate new opportunities—and take better care of yourself while doing so.

Why not...
take one small step toward a cherished goal?

Accept Small Victories

Notice the little victories that make your home life pleasing and satisfying. Instead of dashing here and there, forcing yourself or your mate to reach desired goals (sorting, packing, selling, giving away), focus on a smile, a hug, a word of encouragement, a compliment, and a bit of gratitude toward the other. And start acknowledging yourself as well, whether or not anyone else notices what you do. Pat your own back. Give yourself a small reward: that new book you've been eager to read, a cappuccino with whipped cream on top, an art movie, a new CD. Then, when you least expect it, you're likely to realize just how sweet and cozy your new life really is.

*Make it your ambition to lead a quiet
life, to mind your own business.*
1 THESSALONIANS 4:11

Organize!

Free yourself from household
imprisonment so you can enjoy the rest
of your life in comfort and simplicity.

MARCIA RAMSLAND

Fred and Paulette recently retired and moved downstate from San Jose, California, to Santa Barbara so they could be closer to their only daughter, son-in-law, and granddaughter. They sold their four-bedroom home and now live in a two-bedroom apartment behind their daughter and son-in-law's house. When I spoke with Paulette she seemed overwhelmed. "We have boxes everywhere," she said. "I'm not sure where to begin. I got rid of so many things before we moved, yet here we are with more than we have room for. I'll have to go through everything again."

According to Marcia Ramsland, professional organizer and president of The Organizing Pro & Co., a San Diego-based consulting firm that specializes in helping people get organized, Fred and Paulette are not alone. Ramsland has worked with many couples and individuals who were ready to scale down, to let go of the clutter that filled up their homes and their lives. "I find that people are happier about downsizing when they start early," she says. "As we age it becomes more difficult to manage a large home and all the possessions we've accumulated."

Some people are ready to let go of the ties so they can travel, take up new hobbies, or spend more time with children and grandchildren. But still there is some resistance to the work involved in disposing of a lifetime of possessions and collections. Ramsland encourages those who are sentimental about their furnishings and collectibles to take photos of the things they love. "On the back of each photo jot down the year or the occasion when you purchased the item or received it as a gift." You might even create an album or scrapbook of pictures and commentary. "That way you'll have the memory—without the memorabilia that takes up too much space."

Why not...

pick one area of your home today and purge? Then splurge with small a treat.

Her strategy for successful downscaling comes straight from her experience. People enjoy working with her because, as she's quick to admit, "I once struggled to stay organized. I know what it feels like to be overwhelmed with all the 'stuff' in life."

If you're ready to take Marcia's advice, consider these useful steps to successful downsizing.

- *Take pictures.* Photos should include furniture settings, window treatments, accessories, wall hangings, artwork, and the exterior of your house. The photos will provide a visual inventory of your possessions.

- *Start a notebook.* Use these headings: Hopes and Desires for My New Location, Things to Keep, Items to Dispose Of, Decisions to Make, Family Members' Requests.

- *Work room by room.* Empty the rooms that won't have a counterpart in your new home, such as a garage, basement, or den. Handle those areas first. Then designate one or more of these spaces to separate the things you will sell, give away, or take with you.

- *Label everything.* Place a piece of removable

tape on the back of each item and label it according to its destination: Keep, Toss, Give Away to [name], Sell, and so forth.

- *Clear out closets.* Here is an opportunity to cut down on your moving bill! Don't pay someone to move things you don't want or have forgotten about. Get rid of everything you don't love, like, or use. Take only those items that give you pleasure.

- *Keep it simple.* Get rid of what you don't need or want in whatever way you can. Don't be upset if your children or other relatives decline your treasures. Remember they too have their own tastes and space limits. Be grateful when people do take items off your hands. They're helping you as well as themselves.

Downsizing doesn't have to be a downer. Choose to make it an adventure!

Never be lacking in zeal.

ROMANS 12:11

Practice Delaying Gratification

Patience is the companion of wisdom.

ST. AUGUSTINE

I've become something of an expert at delayed gratification. I don't give in to my urges as quickly as I used to. I pause, think about what I want to buy—whether a fruit smoothie on a hot day or a new outfit for a special occasion—and *choose* to make the purchase when it's prudent and satisfying. I now return home more often with money in my wallet and peace in my mind and heart.

To strengthen this habit I write down in a small notebook the money I spend, whether via cash, check, or debit card. At the end of each week I transfer those numbers to the appropriate category in my expenditures file on my computer: groceries, fuel, medical, restaurants, car wash, clothing, and so on. This seemingly insignificant task has changed my relationship with money.

Why not...
> walk through your favorite store without
> purchasing one thing? Enjoy the sights,
> sounds, and fragrances for what they are.

I'm now completely aware of what I earn, spend, save, and give away. This simple act helps me be more thoughtful about what I purchase. It's given me insights into my emotions and moods and how I've used money in the past (and sometimes in the present) to cope with discomfort and fear.

So window shop to your heart's content. Browse stores, boutiques, and flea markets. Take notes and then go home and see where you stand. Do you *still* want that item? Or can you do without it? Would having it add measurably to your life? If so, then it's okay to go back and purchase it. If not, enjoy the memory of it and move on, grateful to have avoided buying something that would give only temporary pleasure and satisfaction—and likely end up in the discard pile a year from now.

I will listen to what God the LORD will say.

PSALM 85:8

Streamline Habits

I hate housework. You make the beds,
you wash the dishes, and six months
later you have to start all over again.

JOAN RIVERS

Here are some easy and practical streamlining tips to apply if you want to focus on the *up*side of downsizing and create a more cozy feeling in your new digs.

Bedroom

- Buy a colorful quilt that serves as a spread and comforter. When you get up in the morning, pull the quilt into place, fluff your pillows, and—presto!—you're finished making your bed.

- Move the television to another room or, better yet, sell it or give it away. Now that your kids are grown and gone, do you need more than one TV? Probably not. If you want one for guests, put it in the closet until they arrive.

- Clear the tops of your dressers and nightstands. It's easier to clean if you don't have to move stuff to get to the surface. We stash our books in the nightstand drawers, leaving space for a lamp and a small clock on top.

- Organize your closets. Use the services of a company that specializes in such things if necessary. This was the best money we spent when we decided to downsize. Now shoes are on shelves, clothing is hung, miscellaneous items are in cubbyholes. The floor is bare. I can dust or vacuum the space in less than a minute because I don't have to move anything out of the way. Another benefit? I can *see* the clothes and shoes I have and actually wear them instead of shopping for more that adds to the pile.

- Hang photos of you and your spouse, children, and grandchildren around the room. Each morning as you start your day and each night as you go to bed, glance at the pictures and whisper a prayer for each person.

Bathroom
- Purchase one set of towels and use them till

they wear out. I know some people prefer two sets so they can alternate, but think about it. You have to fold and put away the second pair every few days. But if you have only one, just wash and rehang. We bought the highest quality we could find and have been using them for more than three years. They have yet to fray or break down. This might not appeal to you, but it is another way to keep it simple so you have more time for what you really enjoy.

- Place an inexpensive washcloth or small towel on either side of your sink(s). After you wash up and brush your teeth, wipe down the sink, counter top, and mirror. Keeps the area looking nice all week long. Cuts down on deep cleaning and minimizes germs.

- Put away as many tubes and jars and other containers as you have room for. My husband and I each have a drawer to ourselves for our personal items, leaving the counter space free.

Cooking

- Behold the blessing of a Crock-Pot! Put your chicken and veggies, or your beef stew, or other recipe ingredients in this great little time-saver, set the dial, and get on with your day. When it's time to eat, the food is ready!

Why not...

prepare double the amount of food for today's meal so you can enjoy it again tomorrow or the next day?

- Buy bread, rolls, cold cuts, waffles, and so on, and place them in appropriate quantities in plastic bags in the freezer. For example, I purchase a package of eight hot dogs, divide them into four small bags—two in each and then freeze. Take out as needed. No fuss. No mess. No waste.

- Cook enough food for dinner to last for two meals. Prepare four chicken breasts. One night serve two with barbecue sauce; another night serve two with lemon-herb dressing. Add sautéed carrots with one and baked potatoes with the other. Simple side dishes can make each meal seem new. A great way to fool your spouse (or you) who won't eat leftovers.

*Keep your lives free of the love of money
and be content with what you have.*

HEBREWS 13:5

No More Shoulda, Coulda, Woulda!

Your attitude is an expression of your
values, beliefs and expectations.

BRIAN TRACY

I should have known."

"I could have done better."

"I would have made a different choice if I knew then what I know now."

Are these laments as familiar to you as they are to me? Chances are you've proclaimed at least a few in your lifetime. I've had regrets at times, and once in a while a new one will surface. But I'm doing my best to let go of the shoulda, coulda, wouldas since I can't do anything to change the past.

Charles hung a little plaque on the wall near his desk that says, "Freedom is terrifying. It makes you responsible for yourself." How true. We can't be free and guilty at the same time. I'm opting for freedom, which means accepting responsibility for the things I can't change, the courage to change what I can, and the willingness to turn the rest over to God who can renew all of them.

I learned something positive and important from the writings of Brother Lawrence (*The Practice of the Presence of God*), a lay brother who lived in a Carmelite monastery during the seventeenth century. He devoted himself to doing *all* things for the love of God, confessing his sins quickly, and then returning to actions and thoughts that glorified his Lord. He encouraged others not to waste their time going over the missed opportunities, mistakes, and sins. Doing so took precious time away from loving and honoring God.

Why not...

create a list of what you could have or should have done and then cross out every one?

Rather, he suggested, acknowledge your wrongdoings, ask for forgiveness, and then carry on, living a life of simplicity and gratitude, loving God in even the smallest ways, such as sweeping the floor of the monastery kitchen where he performed his daily tasks.

This powerful teaching has helped me drop my

shoulda, coulda, and wouldas to spend the rest of my life expressing my love for God and receiving his love for me so others might see and want to experience this way of life that brings such contentment and clarity of conscience.

Want to join me? Abide in God's comfort and counsel!

Cast your cares on the LORD
and he will sustain you; he will
never let the righteous fall.

PSALM 55:22

Part 7

BUILDING AN INNER LIFE

Growing in Grace

Like any other gift, the gift of grace can be
yours only if you reach out and take it.

AUTHOR UNKNOWN

Thirty years ago I gave my life to Jesus Christ as I sat on a bench overlooking the Pacific Ocean near my home in San Diego. I was a broken woman at age 42, divorced from my first husband, about to marry my second, separated from two of my children, and in the doghouse with my father, who was disappointed that I had walked away from the faith and lifestyle he'd taught me.

But my heavenly Father stepped in and rescued me. Since then I have stayed close to the Lord. I never want to go back to the life I lived before I truly knew him. I can't say living for him has been easy, but I can say it has been completely satisfying. I know that my Redeemer lives—and he lives in me.

Had it not been for the grace of God I wouldn't

be here today in a happy second marriage, in good relationships with my adult children, reconciled to my earthly father before he died, and grateful for every breath I take. So when I think of what it means to grow in grace and to stay close to God over the long haul, one verse in the Bible springs to mind immediately:

> The fruit of the Spirit is love, joy, peace, patience, kindness, goodness, faithfulness, gentleness and self-control (Galatians 5:22-23).

What does it mean to live in the fruit of the Spirit as we continue our journey as mature Christians? Here are some thoughts to consider.

- *Love.* When I think of my husband, children, and grandchildren, the first thing that comes to mind is how much I love them. I care about their lives, their needs, their happiness. I'd do just about anything to ensure their well-being. That's how God is toward you and me and every one of his children. God *is* love.

- *Joy* and *peace.* God assures us that if we follow him he will lead us in joy and peace. My friend Annetta Dellinger refers to herself as "the Joy

Lady." You can't be around Annetta for long without experiencing a "joy burst" for Christ, as she calls it. As a veteran speaker and author, she helps new and mature Christians continue their journeys with joyful countenances and a joyful attitude in all things.

- *Patience.* I'm not a naturally patient person. I like things to happen *now*. I remember when we put our condominium on the market prior to moving to a new city. We scheduled open houses every weekend for six months. Hundreds of people trooped through our home, but no one made an offer. Then one day we decided to make our move, trusting God to make the sale in our absence.

  The night before the moving van pulled up in front of our building to load our possessions, we received a call from one of our daughters, saying she was ready to buy a place of her own and hoped our condo was still for sale because she loved it and wanted it.

- *Kindness.* When I think of how kind the Lord is in the little things as well as the big, I'm humbled. I never have to beg for food or rain.

All my needs are met by his gracious hand. So the least I can do is extend my hand with kindness to those around me. And as I do so, the stronger I will become.

♦ *Goodness.* "He's a good man." "She's a good woman." How often we say or hear these words spoken about someone in public life or someone we know. Such a person has moral excellence and virtue. And when we meet a good person we are impressed, since goodness is not common in today's world. My friend and spiritual mentor Fran was such a person. "God is good," she often said. "Stay close to Jesus and everything will be well." And so it is.

Why not...

pick one fruit of the Spirit and deliberately live it today?

♦ *Faithfulness.* Not long ago I heard a woman speak about her marriage. Her husband was an alcoholic and drug addict. She wanted to leave, to admit her mistake in choosing him as her mate, and to make a fresh start. But every time she brought her case before God he told her, "Stay put." And so she has—for nearly 40 years—and everyone who knows her admires her for her faithfulness to God and to her mate. Today the woman and her husband are in a recovery group and making progress in their relationship.

◆ *Gentleness.* When I think of gentleness I think of my Aunt Madeline. I remember spending time at her house as I was growing up. Her kitchen smelled of spice and sugar as she rolled out dough for special cookies and mixed chocolaty batter for her famous cakes. And I remember chuckling when she told me her secret for propping up a cake layer that hadn't risen properly: "I put a couple of vanilla wafers under the side that sags," she said, "and then I make sure when I cut the cake, I take the piece with the wafers. No one will know the difference except the two of us." Madeline taught me more about growing in grace than almost any other person. She was gentle, authentic, and so loving.

◆ *Self-control.* Living in the fruit of the Spirit comes down to living a life of self-control, surrendering ourselves to God and giving him

full reign over every thought, word, and deed.
With the Lord in charge, we can't help but
grow in grace and become the mature Christians we want to be. And our example will
spill into the lives of everyone we meet, helping them do the same in their journeys.

He has shown kindness by giving you rain
from heaven and crops in their seasons.

ACTS 14:17

Enrich Your Spirit
Through Reading

Today a reader, tomorrow a leader.

MARGARET FULLER

Several years ago I walked into a Christian bookstore in my neighborhood to browse. I was looking for a good book—one that would inspire, encourage, and teach me new things to enrich my relationships with God, my family, and other people. The aisles bulged with shelves, and the shelves bulged with titles! I wasn't sure what to buy.

As I walked from one end of the store to the other, one section captured my attention. There on a shelf were newly bound copies of classics by some of the great Christian authors of all time, such as Hannah Whitall Smith, St. Augustine, Teresa of Avila, and many others. Some were published by Barbour Press in a series called The Essential Christian Library. Others were part of Nelson's Royal

Classics, put out by Thomas Nelson Publishers. And the prices were right. Most were under $10 for a hardbound copy.

I scooped up several. I knew it was time for me to return to the classics to review the truths of Jesus' teachings and plumb the experiences and insights of some of the great thinkers across the centuries.

If you're hungry for some meaty reading that will inspire, encourage, motivate, and provide some cozy evenings, I suggest the following titles. Although they're in alphabetical order, they aren't in any particular order regarding what they've taught me or how much I enjoyed them. I've simply pulled the books down from my shelves and present them to you with the hope they'll be food for your soul as they have been for mine.

Absolute Surrender by Andrew Murray (Moody Press). Do you make and break promises over and over to live the surrendered life and then fail to follow through? Do you commit to prayer and personal time with God one day and neglect it the day after that? I know I've done those things. So what is required to live a life of total surrender? Andrew Murray, a late-nineteenth-century church leader, evangelist, and missionary statesman, explains, inspires, and motivates us in plain language on the subject of what it means to surrender to God and what blessings we can anticipate when we do. This slim volume could change your life. It did mine.

Deeper Experiences of Famous Christians, compiled by James Gilchrist Lawson (Barbour Publishing). The object of this book is to bring to readers the deepest spiritual experiences of the most famous Christians of all ages in their own words. From men and women of the Bible, to the great preachers and thinkers of recent centuries, such as D.L. Moody, Charles Finney, Madam Guyon, and George Fox, each expresses himself or herself in unique terms. Yet the deeper experience they share has a common foundation—the baptism or infilling of the Holy Spirit and the experiences that resulted from it. This book is a testimony of how God has done for them abundantly above all they asked for or thought possible (see Ephesians 3:20). And he can and will do the same for us.

Hudson Taylor's Spiritual Secret by Dr. and Mrs. Howard Taylor (Moody Press). This remarkable classic by the son and daughter-in-law of J. Hudson

Taylor, born in 1832 and founder of the China Inland Mission, demonstrates the power of one man when he openly partnered with God to bring the gospel of Jesus Christ to a hurting world. "Hudson Taylor was no recluse," the opening paragraph of the book clearly states. "He was a man of affairs, the father of a family, and one who bore large responsibilities. Intensely practical, he lived a life of constant change among all sorts and conditions of men…" But he was faithful to test all of God's promises and proved with his own life that "it is possible to live a consistent spiritual life on the highest plane." His personal journey written about with honesty and warmth will inspire and encourage even mature Christian readers.

The Christian's Secret of a Happy Life by Hannah Whitall Smith (unabridged, Barbour Publishing). This volume has remained one of the Christian world's favorite books since its first publication in 1870. Smith believed with all her heart that God intended his people to enjoy a happy, blessed life, and she took it upon herself to show readers his path to that happiness. The book overflows with substance for thought and insights from the author's life. It thrilled me to learn that although she was born almost 100 years before I was, we had much in common: womanhood, marriage, motherhood, writing, devotion to Jesus Christ, and a desire to grow and know more of what God has for his people. This is a book you'll want to return to again and again.

The Practice of the Presence of God by Brother Lawrence (Thomas Nelson). Is it possible to have complete union with God, and if so, what does that mean? To seventeenth-century Christian Brother Lawrence, the answer was yes if one becomes aware of God's nearness in the act of daily, active living. His simple message brings a welcome sigh from those who strive and struggle to find God in a life that is a blur of busyness. Brother Lawrence had to learn the very thing he writes about, and that is *practicing* the presence of God by concentrating on him moment-by-moment to the point where he experienced joy and deep satisfaction regardless of the circumstances around him. This book will compel you to commit yourself to such a practice.

Why not...

buy or borrow one of the books on this list and read chapter one?

The Pursuit of God and *The Pursuit of Man* by A.W. Tozer (Christian Publications). These spiritual classics are among my all-time favorites. I agree with Dr. Warren Wiersbe: "Happy is the Christian who reads a Tozer book when his soul is parched and God seems far away." At just such a time in my life, I was introduced to Tozer—writer, preacher, and pastor for 31 years of Southside Alliance Church in Chicago, Illinois. He was proclaimed even in his lifetime a "twentieth-century prophet." The book is "strong medicine, bitter to the taste but potent if taken in contrition and in belief," says William Culbertson, former president of Moody Bible Institute, in the foreword to the book. To the smug he says Tozer's words may be too bitter. Only those who are without hope will benefit. With the force and potency of an electrical storm Tozer delivers his message to a church that has become spiritually flabby and complacent. There is no mistaking his message. The answer to our ills, whether personal or societal, is God.

> *Sow for yourselves righteousness, reap*
> *the fruit of unfailing love, and*
> *break up your unplowed ground.*
>
> HOSEA 10:12

Try Journaling

Journal writing is a voyage to the interior.

CHRISTINA BALDWIN

My life is a mess," I whispered, as I looked across the table at Joe, the pastoral counselor at our church. "I feel disconnected from my husband, anxious about my children, and spiritually...well to tell the truth, I'm dry. I'm having a hard time praying. God feels so far away."

Joe was silent for a moment. Then he caught my attention with something I didn't expect. "Start a journal, a dialogue with God," he said. "Do it today. I think you'll be surprised at how quickly you'll feel God's presence again."

"But I write for a living," I said. "I don't think I have energy to write in a journal too."

Joe didn't let me off the hook.

"Tell God all the things you've told me," he added. "Do it for a month. Then get back to me."

I drove home, grabbed an empty notebook, and began writing.

"Dear God, it's me, Karen. I hardly know where to begin…" I wrote down the things I'd said aloud to Joe. When I finished I had a sense of peace I hadn't felt in a long time.

Then one Sunday, soon after I started my journal, a deacon at church recommended a book he'd been reading called *Dialogue with God* by Mark Virkler. The deacon didn't know anything about my struggle or my new commitment to keep a journal. Or did he? I read the recommended book in two sittings. The author cited many examples in the Bible of God's dialogues with Moses, David, Paul, and others. I realized I too could keep track of the words God spoke to me.

I began this new way of journaling and continued it off and on for more than 10 years. When I skip a day or two because of busyness or illness or travel, I notice the void immediately.

Why not...
  "free write" two pages without stopping?
  Pick up a pen or type whatever comes to
  mind. No rules; just words.

If you've never kept a journal, consider starting one. There is no right way to do one. You can include sketches, drawings, photos, or simply write a few lines or several pages. It's completely up to you. You might also choose a theme for the year. For example, during 1997 I kept a praise journal. I meditated on a praise Scripture each day and then wrote a short, spontaneous prayer on each daily page. My friend Jane says she likes to write love letters to the Lord. "They have helped me experience more intimacy with God," she says.

By varying the focus of each year or month, you'll never be bored. And I'm certain you'll notice a growing connection with the Lord in every area of your life.

> *Then the LORD replied: "Write down the*
> *revelation and make it plain on tablets*
> *so that a herald may run with it."*
>
> HABAKKUK 2:2

Draw Closer to God

What we are is God's gift to us.
What we become is our gift to God.

ELEANOR POWELL

One year my husband and I attended a retreat for Christian artists. It was the most refreshing and stimulating four days we'd shared in a long time. We don't have the time and funds to do something like this every year, but we *can* set aside a half-day or day for a mini-retreat alone or with others in our church family.

For example, a group from church rented a nearby facility on large grounds where we gathered as a community in the morning to pray and sing and discuss a selected topic. In the afternoon, there was time to stroll the walkways, stop and rest in a little gazebo, doze under a big tree, or sit on the grass and read or write. One retreat center we visited had a chapel where we could sit in silence and revel in God's presence.

I've never come away from such a time unrewarded for my efforts to be there. "'Peace, peace, to those far and near,' says the LORD, 'And I will heal them'" (Isaiah 57:19).

Why not consider organizing such an event for your church? Even a lovely hotel with a spacious setting would make a good spot for a retreat. If you or a friend has a large home with a big yard, that too could be used.

My sister and her friends head for the beach once a year for a half-day retreat that includes time to rest, read, discuss, and eat lunch. There are many creative ways to step away from the world if we put our minds and hearts to it.

Connecting with God through his creation is another way to draw closer to him, and to me it's one of the most rewarding. In the summer of 1988, I had an experience that forever changed my relationship with God. One day in late August I was about to ascend Half Dome in Yosemite National Park as part of an all-women's backpacking wilderness trek. To prepare for the trip I had hiked weekly for several months with a group of friends, learned about tents and sleeping bags and stoves and dried food, and discovered how to carry 30 pounds on my back.

The morning of the hike I was nervous and excited. I was ready. I wanted the full experience—with no regrets. So halfway up the steep rock face, I turned around and stood facing out. There was no room for a false step. I held on to the cable for support, and then I took a deep breath and looked.

In front of me, to the sides, up, down, and everywhere I gazed was a visual feast of massive pines hovering over giant cliffs, huge boulders poised among lush greenery, and majestic peaks jutting into the deep-blue sky. I could scarcely take it in. It was so much more than I'd expected.

This is a holy place, I thought to myself. *God is here.*

Why not...

> take a short walk alone and in silence? Feel the presence of the Lord.

You don't have to climb a mountain to draw closer to God. You can go to a neighborhood park or your own backyard with a lawn chair, a sack lunch, your Bible, and a good Christian book or two. Read and pray, think and ponder, listen and watch for the Lord's loving presence so beautifully reflected in his creation.

It takes so little to become more intimate with God. If you're feeling separated, choose today to reach out to him in writing, through his creation, on a mini-retreat, or in whatever way seems right for you.

> *For [the LORD] has not despised or*
> *disdained the suffering of the afflicted*
> *one; he has not hidden his face from*
> *him but has listened to his cry for help.*
>
> PSALM 22:24

Forgiving Others

Forgiveness is almost a selfish act
because of its immense benefits
to the one who forgives.

LAWANA BLACKWELL

I'll never forget the time my friend Angela spotted me across the lawn at my daughter's wedding reception. Much pain and bitterness had passed between us over the course of our friendship. We had let a terrible misunderstanding keep us apart for years, but we finally reconciled. Then, after I was divorced, moved to a new city, became a Christian, and eventually remarried, we experienced another long separation. But *that* day, as our eyes met, we darted between clusters of guests and rushed into a tight embrace.

"Thank you for coming," I said, surprised at the deep affection I felt for her.

"I've missed you," Angela whispered with such emotion I nearly wept.

Conversation was unnecessary as we hugged each other again. Her presence was a gift, and the fact that we hadn't seen each other in a long time made it even more special. She was older, as was I, but also more mellow, wise, and seasoned by the suffering and joy she'd experienced in life.

It was difficult to imagine that at one time I didn't care if I'd ever see her again. I'd decided I was finished with her. She had hurt me deeply, and I wasn't about to forgive her or forget how she had lied to me, manipulated me by twisting the meaning of my words, and then played innocent to those who knew us both.

But God intervened, and his grace washed over me like a fresh spring rain. This happened during a seminar I attended on the healing power of forgiveness. I surrendered to the power of the Holy Spirit that day and released the people from my past that I had held hostage for so long. Angela was among them.

Forgetting what occurred, however, didn't come as easily, as I was to learn over the course of the months following that seminar. I remember my pastor saying one Sunday morning, just when I most needed to hear it, "Every future has a past, and whether we like it or not, God has given us the past as a gift to keep us oriented to our future." When we close the door on the past we hurt ourselves and everyone we love. Pastor Mark reminded us that if we let it, the past could be our guide to present understanding and future behavior. It can also be our *friend* if...

- ◆ we remember Christ died for our sins, as well as the sins committed against us
- ◆ we repent of the choices we made that we didn't have to make
- ◆ we receive God's tender mercy through Jesus Christ

Then we enter the process of becoming holy and being made clean. And we pray for those who persecute us (Matthew 5:44). I have found that it's almost impossible to hold a grudge against someone and pray for him or her at the same time.

Why not...

ask God for the grace to forgive and release the person you're most irritated with...and then do so?

If you are sincere in your desire to forgive yourself and others, you'll not waste time trying to

reconstruct former conversations, explain your posi-
tion, set the record straight, accuse and counter-
accuse, or assign responsibility for who said what to
whom and when and where. Instead you'll be eager
to let go of the emotional baggage, blame, shame,
and the need to be right. Attempts to recreate past
grievances often widen the gap between people
instead of closing it. Focus on healing the wound.
Leave the rest to the Lord, just as he commands.

Wait for the LORD, and he will deliver you.
PROVERBS 20:22

Part 8

LIVING FULLY

Seize and S-q-u-e-e-z-e

Why not seize the pleasure at once;
how often is happiness destroyed by
preparation, foolish preparations.

JANE AUSTEN

Don't just seize the moment, *s-q-u-e-e-z-e* it! I
decided to do this when I realized one day that
I was *putting in* time instead of *living in* the time
I had. I'd wasted many hours obsessing over personality conflicts, income, deadlines, and neighborhood gossip. My new resolve included focusing on
how I could bring joy and peace to others and to me.

I came across a simple set of precepts in an article
that included doing something kind toward myself, doing something thoughtful toward another,
doing something that needed to be done, and giving thanks at the end of each work day.

Instead of merely going through the motions, I
vowed to take on each task with joy and gratitude. I

determined to make a difference in the life of at least one person each day. Want to join me?

Do Something Kind Toward Yourself

Put something inspirational in your bedroom, garden, kitchen, or other spot that is *just for you*. My friend Betty says, "The mountains and rivers give me peace and contentment, so I surround myself with framed photos of my favorite places." When she feels stress, she takes time to breathe deeply, look at the photos, and relax.

Why not...
focus on one good thing in your life today and give thanks?

Do Something Thoughtful for Another

Brenda has what she calls a "meatball ministry." For the past 20 years she has been making a double batch of her favorite meatball recipe and giving half to a friend or acquaintance, a neighbor with cancer, a new mother home from the hospital, a widower, and so forth. "It's amazing how a few pounds of hamburger meat can minister to those in need," she says.

Do Something That Needs to Be Done

Nagging tasks get easier when you start the day with a small kindness. So do something that needs to be done—even if you don't feel like it. You're likely to notice more energy and a greater desire to tackle other projects you've been putting off. How about phoning people you'd rather not speak to, writing that note asking for forgiveness for a hurt, or taking a bag of clothing to a mission?

Give Thanks Each Day

Someone once encouraged me to make gratitude a regular part of my day by writing down on small slips of paper what I'm most thankful for and then placing the papers in a bag or basket on my desk. This changed my life! Consider becoming the "gratitude guru" in your home or neighborhood. Be quick to say thank you and then, at the end of the day, jot down the blessings you've received.

> *Delight yourself in the LORD and he*
> *will give you the desires of your heart.*
>
> PSALM 37:4

Talk It Out

*If we could all hear one another's
prayers, God might be relieved
of some of his burdens.*

ASHLEIGH BRILLIANT

We know we *should* pray together," said Marge, her face blooming pink as she admitted that she and her husband, Rod, have good intentions but poor follow-through. "We're retired but we're not on the same schedule. My mother lives with us, and she has constant needs. Before I know it, another week has passed and Rod and I haven't gone to God together over anything."

The other husbands and wives in the room added their thoughts and challenges to praying together as our marriage support group started. Charles and I could relate to everyone's stories. For many years our daily routine was a blur of busyness, trying to get out the door for work or, in my case, down the hall to my home office for a day of writing. We always seemed to need to drop out something: a nourishing breakfast, exercise, time to talk, prayer. On the days we made it to the gym, prayer got left out. When we prayed, there didn't seem to be enough time to take power walks or sit and discuss pressing matters.

One day as we were walking along the beach engrossed in conversation about something that needed handling, I remarked, "We really should pray about that before making a decision."

"You're right," Charles said. "I'll pray while driving to work."

We finished our walk, hurried home, showered, ate, and went our separate ways. Then it hit me! Why wait until *later* to pray? We could start walking *and* praying—taking care of two items on our list at the same time. What a concept! I proposed the idea to Charles and he liked it. The next day we started a routine that has become an important element in our marriage: prayer walks. The practice of combining physical and spiritual exercise perked up our relationship immediately.

Praying out loud in front of each other also brought new understanding to our relationship. I began to hear things from my husband I hadn't known before. He had fears about income and concerns for his adult children because of his mistakes when they were young. I heard shame and guilt. These intimate, self-disclosing moments helped me become more compassionate toward him and more alert to ways I could encourage him.

As we continued I felt the freedom to reveal some of my frailties that had been carefully shielded by my outgoing personality. It was such a relief to let down my guard and be honest with God and with my husband.

People began noticing our closeness and commenting on it. One of my daughters said we seemed mellower and more connected to one another. It was true that we were feeling more intimate with each other, but more important, we felt closer to God because as a couple we were in communion with him every single day.

Why not...
walk around the block and pray aloud with your mate or a friend today?

Perhaps best of all is the continual openness of our communication with God and with ourselves. We have been stripped of our pretenses. No more fancy "word feasts," no self-conscious mumblings, no rattling on for the sake of hearing ourselves speak. Like Clement of Alexandria, we'd discovered through experience that "prayer is conversation with God."

If you want to experience more vitality, more joy, and more closeness with your mate, perk it up with a prayer walk! Here are some general guidelines to help you establish this wonderful together time.

- Choose a walking route that suits your style and the time you have.

- Dress for comfort; wear good walking shoes.

- Make walking and praying a habit.

- Take turns praying aloud. Really listen to each other.

- End with a coffee break, a body stretch and cool down, a word of praise and thanks, or all three.

You will call upon me and come and
pray to me, and I will listen to you.

JEREMIAH 29:12

Speak from Your Heart

Truth is the only safe ground to stand on.

ELIZABETH CADY STANTON

The phone rang just as I was pouring soup into bowls and pulling hot rolls from the oven.

"Karen, hi. I hope I didn't catch you eating dinner," a woman said.

"Oh no," I lied. "I have a few minutes. Who's this?"

"Luann," she replied. "Remember me? I met you on a hike last year."

Of course. Instantly I recalled her face and her infectious laugh. "How nice to hear your voice," I said as I juggled the phone with one hand and the soup with the other.

"I'm starting a home-based clothing business," she said. "Could you come to my house next Saturday? I'm going to introduce the line to some of my friends, and it would be a great chance to see you again."

I wanted to say yes so she wouldn't be disappointed. At the same time I wanted to say no so I wouldn't put myself in a bind. I had promised myself no more social engagements until I finished my latest writing project. Then I thought of a third option. I could tell her I'd call her back after I checked my calendar. Still another idea occurred to me. Say yes and see how it goes. Maybe it would work out. I could always call and cancel the day before.

Lies, lies, and more lies. Why can't I just speak the truth from my heart? A moment passed. Finally, I did speak the truth, thanks to the grace of God! And Luann was fine with it. As I look back on my life, I see many other such nooks and crannies where the dust collects, where I cut corners, where I close my eyes to the "white" lies.

But a life of holy boldness demands more than merely getting by. It requires that we keep our word. It's duty in the highest sense. Duty to God, to ourselves, and to others. When we say what we mean and then do what we say, we honor the Lord, show respect for others, and lay a foundation of accountability that helps keep us faithful to God's truth regardless of the circumstances. When you're tempted to be casual with your word, consider these steps from Scripture:

- ◆ *Pray earnestly.* "When you pray, go into your room, close the door and pray to your Father, who is unseen. Then your Father, who sees what is done in secret, will reward you" (Matthew 6:6).

- ◆ *Walk with integrity.* "In everything set them an example by doing what is good. In your teaching show integrity, seriousness and soundness of speech" (Titus 2:7).

- ◆ *Speak the truth.* "Do not let any unwholesome talk come out of your mouths, but only what is helpful for building others up according to their needs, that it may benefit those who listen" (Ephesians 4:29).

Sometimes we don't keep our word because we can't. Something happens. You plan an event and suddenly there's a death in the family. You promise a daughter you'll babysit her children and then you come down with the flu. You sign up for a committee at church and realize down the road you're overcommitted and can't go through with it. What then?

Why not...
> think before you speak—and commit to
> doing this every morning?

Don't let guilt or embarrassment compound the problem. If you can't attend the event or honor the commitment, go to the person and explain. Ask for forgiveness if that's appropriate. To share openly, to keep our promises, and to express ourselves honestly are all worthy goals as long as our hearts are focused on the Lord and his plan for us rather than on our need for approval.

We are not lost or alone when something interrupts our plans. We can call on the Holy Spirit to lead and guide us. His grace and courage will help us make fresh starts when necessary. Hopefully we'll realize how important our words are so we'll be more thoughtful about the ones we choose, and use, and give as we commit to the *up*side of living during the second half of our lives.

> *I tell you that men will have to give*
> *account on the day of judgment for*
> *every careless word they have spoken.*
>
> MATTHEW 12:36

Become an Encourager

Remember, man does not live
on bread alone: sometimes he
needs a little buttering up.

JOHN MAXWELL

Are you the life of the party? The leader? The orderly one? The one who brings a balanced outlook? Whatever your personality, God can use you to encourage others. Consider the gifts you have been given and decide how you can best give in a cheerful way.

"I miss you." "Let's talk." "God loves you, and I do too." "Let's pray together." "May I help?" Such words of kindness and encouragement are important to all of us. Get together with those God leads you to and share the caring words you both long to hear. The Holy Spirit will guide you, and hopefully you'll both walk away uplifted.

Why not...

offer a supportive shoulder to someone in
need today?

A small gift, a loving touch, a drop-in visit. It's
amazing how what we give, whether small or great,
can bless others with encouragement and hope. God
has promised that as we give, so he will give back
to us. What a beautiful remedy for our own needy
hearts! The prayers of a righteous friend truly avails
much more than we can imagine or hope for.

I encourage you to be there when someone
needs a friend to lean on, a shoulder to cry on, a
sister or brother in Christ to share with. And when
you're in need, the Lord will bring such a person
to you. God is committed to encouraging us by
yielding a harvest of friendship, love, support, and
prayer, so let's share his love and commitment with
the people around us.

Each man should give...not
reluctantly or under compulsion
for God loves a cheerful giver.

2 CORINTHIANS 9:7

Mentors Are Gifts from God

*We can do no great things, only
small things with great love.*

MOTHER TERESA

My father-in-law Charlie Flowers taught me a great deal, though I doubt he intended it or knew it at the time. I met him after he and his wife, Ada, had sold their large family home, downsized to half a small duplex, and gave up their car. Life shifted, becoming simple and quiet. Charlie tended his beautiful rose garden; Ada kept up the house and made award-winning pies, especially when my husband and I came to visit.

They were a wonderful example of what it means to live on the *up*side of downsizing. I remember how warm and cozy I felt relaxing in an old recliner in the living room with a handmade quilt tucked around me while we watched television, leafed through old photo albums, or sipped hot tea with honey from dainty china cups. Their lifestyle, free of the cares of prior years, looked good to me during a time when I was still striving to earn a living, helping my kids grow up, and working on my new marriage.

Charlie Sr. loved to tell stories, and whenever he embarked on one, I pulled my chair a little closer. I knew I'd find a pearl or two of wisdom if I listened closely. I remember one time in particular.

"It was Black Tuesday in 1929," Charlie began. He had planned to withdraw some cash from his bank account the day before but he got busy doing chores and didn't make it to the bank before closing time. "I'll go first thing in the morning," he told his wife. But the next day it was too late. The stock market had crashed, and many banks closed for good, including the one he used.

Later that day he met his friend Miles in the street. Charlie told Miles what had happened. On the spot Miles reached into his pants pocket and pulled out $700 in cash. "It's all I've got in the world," he said. "But you've got nothing, Charlie. Here, half is yours." He peeled off $350 and placed it in Charlie's hand. "And you don't owe me a penny."

My husband and I looked at each other in dismay as Charlie continued. How could a few hundred dollars make such a difference? Yet it did. But more important, here were two friends who stood together in the worst of times and moved forward in hope, sharing what they had and trusting God for the rest. What faith and friendship!

I also learned from my friend Fran who mentored me during my early years as a Christian. When we met she was 70 years old and I was 42. I discovered she had been praying for my husband and me long before Fran and I met in person. My daughter had put our names on the prayer list at the church Fran attended, the church that was to become ours as well. She'd been a friend to me in the Spirit first and then in flesh-and-blood when I needed one.

Fran and her husband were retired during that time, and she spent her days loving others through visits, prayer, counsel, and care. She never looked at the downside of life. She was always up, up, up to the opportunities God put in front of her. And here I am, 30 years later, still learning from her example.

Why not...

get together with a person you respect to talk and pray? Call him or her today.

I learned from Grace and Rob too. Grace was

a counselor, minister, and college professor. When she and her husband, a retired physician, downsized from their family home and moved to a retirement complex, Grace carried on with her work until one day she felt the Lord asking her to surrender it all. She was to sit in the back pew of the church on Sunday mornings for six months and simply *pray.* She said it was one of the greatest challenges she faced— no longer in charge, running the show, or teaching others how to live. But after only a few weeks, a cozy glow came over her, a feeling of peace during this later season of life. *Prayer* was her gift, the one God wanted her to exercise. And she did.

Now that I'm in a similar stage of life, I'm realizing that my most peace-filled, happy, and serene moments are when I am praying. Little did I know till now that one of the upsides of downsizing my life would be more opportunities to pray. And so I am grateful for Charlie and Ada and Fran and Grace and Rob, who all lived in front of me and taught me by example.

> *Blessed is he who has regard for the weak;*
> *the Lord delivers him in times of trouble.*
>
> Psalm 41:1

Share Your Gifts

Hide not your talents.
They for use were made.

BENJAMIN FRANKLIN

I don't think I have any talents," my mother once said, mulling over the many gifts she saw in her children. She paused for a moment and then added, "Well, maybe I'm a good listener. Is that a gift?"

"Yes, Mom, it is. And I know it because you've always listened to me, and it's a gift every time."

My mother is now in heaven, but this scene comes to mind as I write. Mom had many talents that she took for granted or overlooked because they came to her with such ease: hospitality, generosity, and a helping hand. Our home was a "happening place" for many friends and family members over the years.

If, like my mother, you wonder what gifts you have, here are some questions to ask to help you uncover them and then use them in positive ways.

What Do I Love to Do?

When I ask myself what I love to do, the answers pop up without thought. I love to write, teach, and speak. Look at the activities and interests you love and explore them further. How about sharing your talent with your community by joining a group with the same interests? If you enjoy gardening, why not beautify public areas with flowers as my friend Lynn does? Do you grow vegetables in your garden? Share your harvest with your neighbors or donate some of your bounty to a food bank. Do you have an interest in politics? Knock on doors and let people know what's going on. Do what you love, and you will live a happier and more satisfying life.

What Am I Good At?

Maybe some of the things you're good at you've overlooked. My neighbor Mike is a great backyard chef. This year he shared it with those who live close by. People put together a potluck for the Fourth of July, and Mike bought, marinated, and barbecued the best ribs I've ever eaten. I can still taste his homemade sauce. He's agreed to be the community chef for our neighborhood celebrations from now on.

What Comes Naturally to Me?

What do you do almost without thinking? What comes so easily you might miss it? My friend Terri is a natural-born leader. She loves the wilderness and has been leading hikes and backpacks and car camps for years. Everyone who joins her has a rich experience that includes hiking, eating great food outdoors, and sitting around the campfire singing songs and playing games.

Why not...
share your talents? However small or insignificant they may seem, God will use them.

Consider what you do naturally. Do you play a musical instrument? Join the worship team at your church or a community orchestra or band. You could perform at parties and wedding receptions, reunions and family events—and maybe even earn a little money on the side.

Do you have counseling or teaching skills that are second nature? You could lead a Bible study, a children's church class, a study group for teens or single mothers or seniors.

What Do People Say They See in Me?

Finding your talents might be as simple as paying attention to what others say about you. When you're asked to host an event, participate in a cause, write a short article for a newsletter, take photographs for a friend's party, sit with a sick grandchild, arrange a bouquet of flowers, or set up a website for an organization you believe in, think about what this says about you.

We don't have to sit in high places and have great authority to make differences in people's lives. We just need to spread the love of God by using the gifts and talents he entrusted us with.

> *[The person who delights in the*
> *LORD] is like a tree planted by streams*
> *of water, which yields its fruit in*
> *season and whose leaf does not*
> *wither. Whatever he does prospers.*
>
> PSALM 1:3

Karen O'Connor

*Opening hearts and connecting lives
through writing and speaking*

Karen has authored many magazine articles and books, including the bestselling *Gettin' Old Ain't for Wimps*. She's won numerous awards, including the Paul A. Witty Award for short story writing (International Reading Assoc., 2005). A sought-after speaker, Karen enthusiastically and humorously inspires people to...

- experience and express more joy and gratitude
- embrace positive growth
- achieve greater intimacy with God, self, and others
- polish communication and leadership skills

For more information about Karen, her books, her speaking, or to share with her why you believe the golden years are great, contact:

Karen O'Connor Communications
10 Pajaro Vista Court
Watsonville, CA 95076

Phone: 831-768-7335
Email: Karen@KarenOconnor.com

in the heart of Peace

C. R. Gibson®

FINE GIFTS SINCE 1870

All images © Hulton Getty Picture Collection
Design by Keith Jackson
Picture research by Jon Wright
All text, unless otherwise attributed, by Jonathan Bicknell

Developed by Publishing Services Corp., Nashville, Tennessee.

Published by C. R. Gibson®
C. R. Gibson® is a registered trademark of Thomas Nelson, Inc.
Nashville, Tennessee 37214
Printed and bound by L. Rex Printing Company Limited, China

ISBN 0-7667-7596-8
UPC 0-82272-47484-0
GB 102

in the heart of Peace

"By three
things will a
nation
endure —
Truth, Justice
and Peace."

"Pause a while. For if you rush with noise and fury you will miss the moment."

"I am a child
of peace..."

"...And am resolved to keep the peace for ever with the whole world..."

"...Inasmuch as I have resolved it at last with my own self."

Johann Wolfgang van Goethe

"And the challenge can be conquered. So take heart."

"Let the cares
of yesterday
settle.
Today is a
new day."

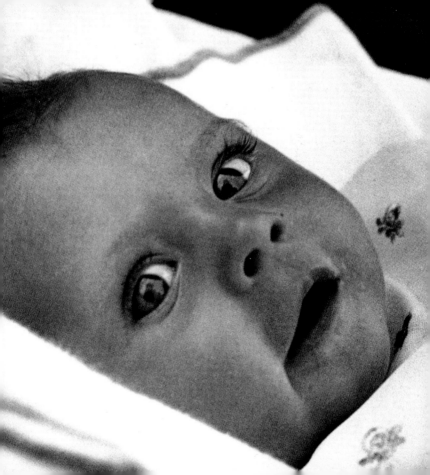

"All things come to those who wait."

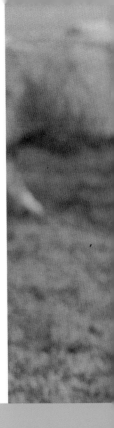

"Come away,
Come away
and come
closer to the
peace."

"Like a bird in the forest whose home is its nest, my home is my all, and my center of rest."

John Clare

"'Don't you worry and don't you hurry' I know that phrase by heart, and if all other music perish, it would still sing to me."

Mark Twain

"My heart is
at rest within
my breast
and everything
else is still."

"Peace is indivisible."

Maxim Litvinox

"O God grant me the courage to change what I can and the patience to endure what I cannot."

B. J. Gupta

"Silence is golden."